To Peter & Hilda

en memo

Love

Miranda Word -

Fedorowich

WINDOWS AND PENCIL SHARPENERS
The Story of One Man's
Journey through Disability

Miranda Ward
with Len Hart

*This book is dedicated to
the memory of Jack Ward*

Contents

WINDOWS AND PENCIL SHARPENERS:
The Story of One Man's Journey through Disability

iUniverse books may be ordered through booksellers or by contacting:

iUniverse
1663 Liberty Drive
Bloomington, IN 47403
www.iuniverse.com
1-800-Authors (1-800-288-4677)

ISBN: 978-1-4917-6441-1 (sc)
ISBN: 978-1-4917-6442-8 (e)

Library of Congress Control Number: 2015904879

Print information available on the last page.

iUniverse rev. date: 05/13/2015

Introduction

The story of Jack William Ward is a tale of fun and adventure, of sweat and tears, of heartbreak and renewal, of illness, near death and new life, of faith, hope and love, and finally eternal life.

The author of this story is an amateur to say the least, but the subject of the story was a champion. He was a champion in his recreation and in his work, in health and in his illness, in his new life and even in his death. He lived the whole of his life filled to the fullest measure. When he played, he played hard; when he fought, he fought hard; and, later in life when he worshiped, he worshiped with his entire being. He had a way of giving credit where credit was due and, when it was required, of taking responsibility for his actions. This champion had a tough life, but he always toughed it out, and he did so with integrity. This champion was my husband of over ten and a half years.

Being born with learning disabilities made life difficult, but not impossible, and he proved that each step of the way. And along the way he did manage to accomplish most of the things that he set out to do. The objective of this book is to show Jack's character and his willingness to overcome the many obstacles in his life. When someone said "you can't", he set out to prove he could.

This is not his complete biography. It is a story that proves some people do figure out how to work life in spite of the hand they are dealt. Jack figured it out.

Hopefully this story will also show how to deal with the spiritual side of life. Jack wanted me to tell that side too. He became a great believer in God and the power of prayer. One thing his mother did for him in his early years was to insist that he go to Sunday School at the Anglican Church. This was a natural choice because his father, coming from England, was High Anglican. He later joined the Scouts in a United Church which he decided on his own to attend for awhile. He also went to a Baptist Church for a short time, but that ended when he was asked to play Joseph in a Christmas pageant where the part of Mary was played by a girl he did not like.

Jack loved life. He never had a dull moment that he did not know how to fill. When all else failed he talked. He talked to everybody who would listen. When there was no one to listen he talked to himself. He did not usually complain about much, but he could tell you how he would run City Hall if given the opportunity. He loved to talk politics. Often his talk turned to a good joke in order to make someone laugh. He seemed to feel that was his calling in life.

Jack was also a collector. He collected all kinds of stuff. As we progress with his story it will become obvious that much of it is written either by stories he told or by things he collected and preserved so that when I would find them, they would be recorded as a part of the tapestry of his life. It was only after his passing that I became fully aware of all the material he had gathered over the years. There was volume after volume of material, much of it immaterial, but still enough pertinent content to make this narrative a possibility. Jack always felt that someday the things he collected would not only prove useful, but necessary.

Some would say that Jack collected too much, but to him it was the same concept as preserving some endangered species. He collected stamps, old videos and records, pens from everywhere (including one from Stephen Juba, a Winnipeg mayor from the '70's), some that would write and others that wouldn't, shelves and shelves of books, and stacks of other "stuff". He had a fifty-seven volume set of Zane Gray books that no one ever read. He also had a couple of other sets of books that came into his possession after his mother died that she had apparently treasured. Each set contains four children's books. One set was published by the Samuel Lowe Company in the early 1940's. The other set was printed in the late '30's or early '40's and has Litho USA on the back cover. This second set has the oddest pages. Each page is only partially complete with the pictures and stories being spread over more than just one page. Both sets are in such good shape that I doubt if they were ever handled by a child. Perhaps they were books that Jack's mother read to him when he was young, but there are no names in the books that would give away their secrets.

Sometimes his obsession to collect led to

frustration, especially when he saved for posterity something that was needed today. One such thing was a letter that I had received from a doctor's office in response to an inquiry that I had made. I am sure that I never even seen the correspondence as the return address would definitely have caught my attention. It was partly opened but never taken out of the envelope. Many times I wished I had heard something back about this particular issue, but I was never made aware of the reply to my inquiry. Now the answer was in his files almost ten years later. I don't know what to make of this. I know he would not have deliberately kept the letter from me. It was just another one of those moments when he saw something that had to be kept. He put it away and unknowingly left me to wonder why these people had never responded to my letter. At any rate, this book would not have been possible without Jack's compulsive drive to collect.

Chapter 1 Secretive Birth

Jack William Ward was born in Brandon, Manitoba on May 21, 1938. Nothing is known of the first five years of his life except that those years were spent in the city of his birth. It is speculated that he lived in a home by special arrangement during this time, although he had no memory of it.

At the age of five Jack was said to have been adopted by his parents, the newlyweds William Henry Ward and Lucille Mildred Grover. William or "Billy", a British citizen, had just returned from England after completing his service in the British military. He had made a previous visit to Canada in 1937 during which time he had become acquainted with Lucille. Upon his arrival in Winnipeg, the couple married and traveled to Brandon to pick up their adoptive son.

At least, this is the story that was told. There is no immediate record of Jack's birth or of an actual adoption. Nor was there any trauma usually associated with adoption or the search for biological parents that is frequently undertaken by an adopted child. It appears that they were a quite well adjusted small family of three. In trying to piece things together it can be speculated that the couple was more than just slightly acquainted when they first met in 1937. The result could have been a pregnancy, possibly unknown to the couple until after William returned to England. A family friend remembers that Lucille made frequent trips to

Brandon and that one in particular had been for a prolonged period of time. Therefore, it is possible that Lucille, finding out that she was in "the family way" had traveled to Brandon to keep her condition a secret. After the baby was born, she made arrangements to keep her son in Brandon, visiting him frequently, until William could return and make her an honest woman. After this was accomplished, they traveled to Brandon to collect their son and then returned to Winnipeg with the story of his adoption. They validated this story by informing friends and family that they were unable to have children of their own. This may well have become reality after Jack's birth as Jack, adopted or not, was the only child that William and Lucille were to have.

There are reasons why this all had to be kept such a secret. One must remember that this was the 1930's. Illegitimate births were highly frowned upon. They were the titillating subjects of gossip and as such a huge embarrassment to the family and a perpetual slur upon the mother and her offspring. And Lucille was not a young girl. She would have been well aware of the societal consequences. In addition, Jack's father came from Sheffield, England and there is some evidence that he was a Master Mason. He was forty years old when Jack was born, as it is assumed, out of wedlock. It is doubtless that such behavior would have been unacceptable for a man in his position. At any rate, after his return to Canada, his marriage to

Lucille and the addition of Jack to the family, his contact with members of his family and social circle were minimal.

Before her death at 84 Lucille admitted to Jack that she had given birth to him. She also gave him a little locket with a picture of him at about eighteen months of age on one side and a picture of his father on the opposite side. I think that he had always suspected this. There was so much family resemblance. It would have been hard to miss. And yet Lucille's best friend adamantly advised me that Lucille could not have children and that Jack was definitely adopted. This she said she knew for sure. At the time the lady was ninety five years old, so I didn't challenge her despite our belief to the contrary.

Chapter 2   Growing Up

After Jack's parents married in 1943 and completed their family by "adopting" Jack, they settled in the Brooklyn area in the northwest part of Winnipeg. William worked for the Canadian Pacific Railroad (CPR) at the Weston Shops in North Winnipeg, the main repair depot for the railway.

It is said of war veterans that they either marry and have families in an attempt to resume normal living or they become alcoholics in order to drown the horrors of war. Jack's father was a veteran of two world wars and he did both.

Jack's parents consumed a lot of alcohol over the years. He said they partied every weekend. His mother told him once that she had always drank. Did this mean she drank during her pregnancy too? This could account for some of Jack's problems; maybe most of them. Many of the same symptoms of Fetal Alcohol Spectrum Disorder (FASD) were present in Jack's life.

Why he never picked up the habits of his parents is a marvel to me. It would have been easy for him to have slipped into the same lifestyle, but Jack made other plans for his life. He was determined to show people that he could be what they thought he could never be. He made deliberate choices that helped him get to where he wanted to go, and smoking and drink would have gotten in the way. And somehow, somewhere in his life he did accomplish most of the things he had set out to do.

Sometimes he arrived at them almost too late, but he did get there.

Jack said he believed that he was spared from some things because he felt that, even though he was not aware of it, God had always had His hand on his life to protect him from various pitfalls. More than once he was spared from accidents. As a young teen he got hit by a car and walked away unscathed. The driver of the car called his mother to see how Jack was and she said he was just fine and that he had gone to bed. "Why all the questions?" she asked. He told her he had hit Jack with his car that day and he was sure that Jack must have been hurt, but that he had gotten up and ran all the way home before the guy could check him out.

Another time, he was hit by a bus while riding his bicycle. He was thrown clear, but his bike was a write off. He was never able to figure out how that happened. Later he came to understand that God has a plan for your life and that He will go to great lengths to make sure it is completed. That is, if you are at all willing to surrender your life to Him. At the time Jack was unaware of such things, but he was always willing.

I don't believe that Jack was ever officially diagnosed with learning disabilities as a child. No one ever told him that he had ADD (Attention Deficit Disorder) or that he had dyslexia. Nor did anyone ever come alongside him to help him. He was raised in a time when no one looked for reasons why a child underperformed and those with learning disabilities usually fell through the cracks. But these were things that I recognized in Jack during our many years of friendship prior to our marriage. Without taking these things into account, it would have been very difficult for a teacher to instruct such a child. And since Jack was never properly diagnosed, his school years were deemed a failure.

It is no wonder then, that there are stories told about the many things he did as a child. After all, he was not considered to be very bright by his home or at school. His father and his teachers called him names a child should never be called. But it seemed that instead of being damaged for life, he became more resourceful in his attempts to overcome his shortcomings. He developed a definite need to prove them all wrong, and he became adept at doing so.

Chapter 3   Windows and Pencil Sharpeners

Shortly after we were married I noticed something peculiar about Jack. He would never stay sitting with me when we went to church. He would start out beside me as if he had good intentions, but he never stayed. Being newlyweds, this kind of behavior perplexed and frustrated me. Why did he not want to sit with his new wife? He would remain with me for the singing, but as soon as the speaker got up he was usually gone. From this I assumed he did not want to hear the message. For a few years this thoroughly puzzled me. Because of the way the Baptist Church we attended in Winnipeg was set up, I could not observe what he was doing in the back.

When we first moved to Portage la Prairie we attended a very conservative Baptist church. His nomadic roaming in the rear of the sanctuary was not appreciated. It was frowned upon and even questioned. Because of this, he felt prohibited from wandering and so was compelled to sit with me through the entire service. As a result, he soon started to tell me that he was not feeling well in church and frequently he went home before the service was over.

It was during this time that Jack asked to be baptized. To him it was a declaration to the world that he had decided to commit his life to Jesus. Frequently, the next step after baptism is to become a member of the church. But Jack was adamant that we not join, that we rather look somewhere else.

The reason he stated was that I should be involved in some area in the church in order to make use of my Bible College training. Due to the conservative nature of the church and the leadership's assertion that I had attended the "wrong school", we knew that this would not happen. Also, several people commented that we did not seem to be happy and that our basic belief in having freedom in Christ seemed to be eroding.

Consequently, we began to seriously seek out a different church where we could both be more comfortable. We found First Baptist Church in Portage la Prairie where we stayed until after Jack passed on and I moved away in order to be closer to family. When we walked into that church on a Thursday morning to inquire about the assembly, there were only two people there, the secretary and one deacon. As we entered through the front doors and passed into the sanctuary, we both breathed a sigh of relief and said in unison, "We are home."

It was while attending First Baptist that I was able to see for the first time what Jack was doing when he was not sitting with me. We were now in a place where we both felt very much at home and yet he was still not remaining with me through the service. He had yet to explain to me what was going on. Then one day he told me about windows and pencil sharpeners.

Jack had had a problem sitting still in his desk at school. He was distracted by all of the antics of the other students and could not concentrate on what the teacher was saying. I dare say that misbehaving and talking out loud would also have been problems for him. He realized that if he was going to learn anything at all he would have to figure out a way to increase his attention span and so attend to his lessons. He discovered that if he stood by the window and looked outside he could better hear and understand the class lecture. In fact, if he was asked a question while sitting at his desk he could not come up with an answer. However, if he was asked to contribute to the class while standing at the window, he was always ready with an answer.

Jack initially used the excuse that he needed to sharpen his pencil to enable him to go the window, as that is where the pencil sharpener was located. Consequently, he was forever sharpening his pencils. He must have ground his way through a great number of them. Indeed, his mother did worry about all of the pencils she was required to buy.

After awhile, his teachers caught on that while Jack was at the window he was not cutting up in class. Therefore, as long as he behaved, they began allowing him to stand at the window rather than forcing him to sit in his desk.

Learning disabilities were not a hot topic back in the 1940's and '50's. If a child did not attend in class they were considered to be bad kids. But Jack really did want to learn. He wanted his father to be proud of him. And he certainly did not like being called stupid. Jack was determined to do his best to learn and to make people proud of him.

After hearing this story, I began to take note of what he did in church when he was not sitting with me. Sometimes he would sit or stand in the back. Other times he would wander about, but always within earshot of the proceedings. Despite his wanderings, Jack did not forget me. If I had a little cough he would be right there with a glass of water or a peppermint from the supply that he always carried in his pocket. I have come to sometimes wondere if Jack needed a bigger window in church, maybe even one with a pencil sharpener.

Our new church family willingly accommodated him. They designated a chair for him in the back and gave him the job of welcoming any late comers and directing them towards a seat. He was the first to meet and greet any newcomer. And he had a way with children. There was one elderly couple who would bring their great-grandson to church. The boy was quite hyper, but Jack seemed to know how to take control of the situation. At times Jack could get the lad to sit quietly beside him. At other times Jack would end up in the Sunday School class one-on-one with the boy, enabling the rest of the class to go on. Jack understood that child. And thus he became a true asset while he sat or paced in the back of the church.

Eventually, Jack became an official usher and greeter in the church, but he never gave up his chair along the back wall. After his passing I found dozens of little notebooks that he had carried in all his suit pockets and had filled up with sermon notes. When I was preparing to move, someone from the church came to pick up some of my bags of shredded paper. I commented that there were many good sermon in those bags. Most were in his own brand of shorthand and could not be read even before they were shredded. Now I know how he had been learning all the while he was roaming around in the back or just watching the door.

Jack was never a good student, but it did not follow that he never got anywhere in life. He worked hard to overcome his inabilities often through unconventional means that seldom made sense to the rest of the world around him. He knew that anything could be accomplished if you maintained a positive attitude and never gave up. He was frequently misunderstood, but those few who took the time to get to know and appreciate him were repaid with years of kindness and loyalty.

Chapter 4   Difficulties

Writing this account was supposed to be easy. Jack had promised that he would be here to help interpret his poor handwriting, to give the intent behind the materials he saved, and to basically facilitate in the compilation of his stories. But, that was then and this is now. He passed away before I had a chance to make any great sense of his scribblings.

I was left with the task of going through about forty or more huge binders full of material. This was daunting in and of itself, but attempting to decipher his peculiar penmanship, to make sense of his original spelling of words, and to follow the flow of his ideas made the task nigh unto impossible. Reading his books did become somewhat easier as I became more familiar with the way he thought and expressed himself. At times, it was if I could read his mind.

Now, I am so grateful that he told me so many of his stories, some more than once. He had an amazing memory and he loved story telling. He was truly a delight to be around, usually; and his chattering was quite refreshing, most of the time. Sometimes people, myself included, felt that Jack talked too much. He didn't agree. I asked him once why he talked to himself so much. He only half teasingly said that that was the way he got the best answers. I know that he talked and wrote himself through many trials in life.

His writings are full of good advice to himself and information that he garnered from other people and various sources he happened upon. His books also contained many of his stories, accounts of life with God on his side, writings about marriage, his famous Jack's Jokes pages, and his pre-Christmas write-ups which I used each year to help him do up his Christmas letters. Christmas 2013 was his twenty-third consecutive Christmas letter and it received rave reviews. It spoke so well as to who he was that I used it as his eulogy at his memorial service.

Now many of the things he collected have become useful in constructing his story. So did some of the artifacts he had saved from his parents, as well as the many newspaper clippings and the pictures he preserved among his own ramblings.

As I skimmed through all his books, shredding thousands of pages of irrelevant or indecipherable materials, I frequently would encounter my name or the words, "Tribute to My Wife". I kept those pages. Some were really quite good. None ever contained a single negative word about me. I know I am not perfect, but he chose to never dwell on the negatives. He loved to live life on a positive note.

To show you a bit of how his learning disability looked, I have included a sample of his writing as transposed from his scratchings to the typewritten page. Below is one of his tributes to me. I have endeavored to leave the misspellings and grammar intact just the way that he wrote it. Please keep in mind that this is the work of a man who did many things in life quite successfully, including working in a business environment.

A TRUBUTE TO MY-WIFE

SHE A SENSATION LADY (SHE AN SENSATION WIFE) SHE ALLWAY GOT TIME FOR ME OR ANYONE ELSE WHO ASK FOR HER HELP
SHE WAS A FRIEND TO ALL THAT NEED A
FRIEND SHE HAD TIME FOR ME AND SHE HAD TIME FOR YOU THEIRS BEAUTY ALL AROUND US WHEN YOU-HAD MIRANDA FOR A FRIEND
ONE OF THE BEST THINGS GOD HAS GIVEN ME WAS A WOMAN (A GIFT TO ALL MEN TO LOVE) HE GAVE ME THIS GIFT (AND I MARRIED HER)
(WE NEVER APPRECIATE WHAT WE HAVE UNTIL WE LOOSE IT) AND WISPER IN YOUR EAR TELL YOU I LOVE (SHE ONE OF A KIND
KIND HEART-WARM SMILE
THEIR NO JOY-LIKE LASTING LOVE
SHES SUPPORTIVE (SHE HONEST) (SHE CARING)
WE HAVE A COMMON BOND TOGETHER
SHE A DEVOTED WIFE (SHE DEVOTED TO- HER CHURCH AND FAMILY
SHE STRONG AND UNDERSTANDING
SHE HAS LOTS OF LOVE TO GIVE SHE HAS COMPASION FOR EVERY ONE
THEIRS NO TIME LIKE THE PRENCE TO TELL YOU I LOVE GOD HAD ONLY ONE LIKE THIS AND - HE GAVE YOU TO ME
OUR MARRIAGE
JACK AND MIRANDA 2007
MIRAND I CAN'T SAY GOOD NIGHT UNTIL I SAY I LOVE YOU

*MARRIAGE TEACHES TO LISTEN TO EACH OTHER WHEN
ONES TALKING
TO LOVE IS TO LISTEN
TO LISTEN IS TO LEARN
OUR LOVE IS BASED ON COMMON SOURSE
MIRANDA YOUR LOVE IS MY SUNSHINE
THAT KISSES MY CHEEK EACH DAY
GET IN TOUCH WITH YOUR FEELINGS AND
KNOW THAT I AM FELLING MIGHTY LUCKEY TO HAVE A
WIFE LIKE YOU (MIRANDA)THE WARDS, THE
INCREDABLE COUPLE.*

Most of Jack's writings are like this.
Sometimes he would look up words or ask me about
them. At least then he would have the correct
spelling. All of Jack's life his handwriting had been
very poor. This was exacerbated by poor spelling
and by the omission of words from his sentences.
And all was written in large capital letters. His
penmanship did undoubtedly cause his father some
concern. He had voiced his opinion on Jack's
intelligence more than once, and it was not kind.
When Jack's mother passed away we came into a
possession of a letter that had been written by his
father at the age of nineteen. It was written to his
parents at the passing of his grandmother and
explained that he could not come home for the
funeral as he could not get leave from the army. It
was written in the most graceful handwriting that I
have ever seen. I would have thought that it was
written by a woman had it not concluded with a
beautiful, personally inscribed signature. The
difference between Jack's handwriting and his

father's was stark, and it helps to understand some of his father's disappointment in him.

Jack's positive disposition was not reflected solely towards his marriage and me, but to life as a whole; even our illnesses. If I was down about my feeling unwell or about his health, he would remind me that we had been here before and that God had always been there with and for us.

After Jack's decision to follow Christ, he had twelve years to learn about the Christian life. He did this by listening, by observing, and by writing it all down. He would make notes in church, or wherever and whenever he felt he heard something worth remembering. Then, when he came home he would transfer the information into one of his huge binders. Though much of the content was good, some was repeated in several books. His forty plus volumes could easily have fit into five volumes.

In one of the books Jack worked on before going into the hospital for the last time was a four page letter written to me. Some of it was of a quite personal nature, but the main thing he desired to do was to thank me for all the things I had done for him during his cancer years and for what I would yet do for him in the time he had left and after he was gone. He was also kind of apologizing for not being able to stick around for too much longer. I am very thankful I did not find this letter until after he was gone.

There were three words that permeated much of Jack's writings. They are all found in

1 Corinthians 13. They are faith, hope, and love. Those words are so intertwined in his writings that it is quite obvious that in his mind you could not have one without the other two. In one of his books he had printed this entire chapter from Corinthians.

It was in the context of these three words that he wrote many a good piece on Christian marriage, or just what marriage meant to him. He had one failed marriage and he was not about to make the same mistakes again. He studied the concept of marriage. He learned that if you fit the concept of a Christian marriage into 1 Corinthians 13, you should come up with a perfect formula for a good marriage. It really is all there.

With all these tributes he wrote to me as his wife, I feel that it is only fair and right for me to write this book as a tribute to his life and his love as he had requested of me many times. I will always miss him and value the time I spent with him. I learned so much from Jack.

Chapter 5   Wrestling

One of things that Jack loved to talk about was the years that he had been involved in professional wrestling, both as a wrestler himself and also as a promoter. What is it that makes a young man want to wrestle? It must be different for each one, but Jack had a very specific reason.

When Jack was about fourteen his parents took him on a weekend trip to Kenora, Ontario. True to form, his parents spent most of their time inside a bar. As Jack was underage and could not go inside, he hung around outside for a lack of anything else more interesting to do. Unfortunately, a group of local boys came by and mugged him and beat him up quite badly. His parents had no other real choice but to take their son home, but they blamed him for ruining their weekend with their friends. This was a turning point in Jack's life. He decided that weekend that as soon as he could start to work he would join the YMCA and take up wrestling. He wanted to make sure that he was never at such a disadvantage again. If he was going to have to fight, he might as well learn how to do it right so that he could make a good accounting of himself.

After Jack had gone as far in school as he felt he could go, he dropped out and went to work. He had a few mindless jobs until he was forced into the role of the man of the house. Jack's father's smoking and drinking finally caught up with him and he had a massive and disabling stroke. Now Jack needed to get his dad out of bed in the morning, put him in his wheel chair, and then go to work. At noon he would come home for lunch, do some chores for his dad, and then go back to work. In the evening he would put his father to bed. The next day it would start all over again. The family needed the money, and so this became Jack's daily routine.

When the railway saw what had happened to William, they gave Jack a job so that he would be able to make more money. Though he had the responsibility of taking care of his father, he now had the money to join the YMCA and fulfill the promise he had made himself. He began lessons in self-defense and this training eventually led to a wrestling career. Before too long his father was admitted to Deere Lodge Centre in Winnipeg, a hospital for veterans, and he never came home again. He passed away at the age of fifty-nine when Jack was only nineteen.

Soon after his father's death, Jack's mother sold their house, packed up, and moved to Calgary. Lucille had gone to look after her sister's children. But who was to look after Jack? Jack was devastated. He had lost both of his parents in one foul stroke. He had to find a place to live on his own and, with the railway on a strike, a way to provide for himself. He couldn't wait the strike out, so he found a different job -- and continued to wrestle. And soon, he had his own club, the Westbrook

Wrestling Club. and with it a new identity. He now became known as Jack "Killer" Ward.

Jack never conveyed to me many of the details of the founding of his wrestling club. It seems that a group of the guys who were taking lessons at the YMCA decided to step it up a notch and take their passion into various community centers throughout the area. And apparently it was decided that Jack would be their promoter.

As promoter, Jack had assembled a stable of good wrestlers. I did not know him then, but there are a few names that stood out in the stories that Jack used to tell. The original club included John Searcy, Claire Morden, and Wayne Matthews. I have personally met John. He came to visit Jack in the hospital each time that Jack was really sick, including the last time when Jack was in palliative care.

I never did meet Claire Morden, but I came to know his wife Jane. She was a big encouragement to both Jack and me over the years. When we lived at Southport just south of Portage, often the door bell would ring and there would be Jane.

Then there was Wayne Matthews. He was legally blind and the boys in the club were not sure if they wanted a blind wrestler. Jack suggested Wayne take on each of them for one round. If he could take them, he was in; if he couldn't, he was out. Well, he took them all on and came out on top. He was definitely in. Wayne had taken up the sport when he was in the blind institute and he was very good. He was short and fast and anticipated their every move. It is often said that when one of a person's senses are weak, the other senses adapt and become much more acute. Such was certainly the case with Wayne. He was called "Wayne the Magnificent". I don't know who gave him that name, but when he would call Jack and leave a message on our voice mail, he would always identify himself in that way.

After the Westbrook Wrestling Club had become fairly well established they were asked to take a show to Headingly Jail. When they arrived Jack realized that several of his old school chums, the ones who had graduated when he couldn't, were calling his name from behind the bars. They wanted to know why he had never gotten himself in trouble and was still on the outside. They remembered him as the boy least likely to succeed from their school.

This spoke to Jack. And because the community had so heartily supported Jack and the wrestling club, he decided it was time to give something back. He felt that it would be beneficial to open a junior wrestling club in his neighborhood for young boys twelve and up. The members of the senior club could teach the junior boys and so keep them off the streets and out of trouble. I came to know two boys from this group, John Searcy's younger brother Barry and his friend Tom Emms.

Jack decided to take these boys to the big championship games their first year. They lost miserably and some criticism came Jack's way.

Then the very next year these same boys won most of the championship matches in which they wrestled. He then explained to the club that the reason he took them the first year was because, "You need to be a good loser before you can be a good winner." Jack was full of that kind of plain wisdom.

Some of those young men became quite successful in life. Barry Searcy told me that Jack would probably never realize how much he had done for him. I was so proud of my husband when I heard that. These men honored and respected Jack all of his life, even as he lay in the hospital.

It can be said that Jack was not very good with the financial side of things. Money never did mean much to Jack. Once when he was moving he decided that, since it was his, he ought to remove the carpet and take it along with him. When he rolled it up he discovered quite a sum of money that he had placed under the rug for safekeeping some time previous. He had totally forgotten about it. Due to Jack's nonchalance in the handling of money, his old school buddy Art Cheadle became involved as the financial manager of the club.

By now Jack's mother had been in Calgary for quite a while and she decided to return to Winnipeg for a visit. When she arrived in the city she called Jack from the bus depot to come and pick her up. No one answered. She tried calling some of her old neighbors. Again, no one answered. So she called a cab. When she got close to home, she saw where the whole community was. She had come to town on the night that a wrestling match had been scheduled and the entire neighborhood was gathered at her son's club. She knew that Jack wrestled, but she had never imagined that he could be successful in a venture such as this.

Some years later the school division called Jack and asked if he would teach wrestling in their school after hours. They desired to provide an activity to help keep their students off the street. Jack and Wayne agreed to give it a try. For several weeks they attempted to work with the kids, but the boys did not wish to behave. In fact, some of the bigger boys threatened to take them on in the street and to lay a licking on them. With Wayne being blind and Jack now being much older it was not deemed to be a safe sport for them to teach under these circumstances.

Jack never ever planned to fail at anything. If he did happen to fail he would usually just look for a different solution to the problem. But this was one he just had to give up on. It really hit him hard. By this time his first marriage had failed, and now he had to admit defeat again in this sport that he knew and loved so well. I remember him feeling very bad for the kids.

Chapter 6   Square Dancing

Jack's mother could see with her own eyes that Jack was a wrestler. Beyond that, she didn't believe him to be all that coordinated. Dancing was not considered an option in his upbringing. And besides, she was convinced that her son was born with two left feet. In fact, Jack rarely stopped long enough to do things gracefully. He was more like the proverbial bull in a china shop.

But then Jack discovered square dancing and he fell in love with the art. He decided that this was something that he must learn. He continued to wrestle, but now he added this new form of expression into his life. The perceived inconsistency in these activities -- that he would wrestle one night, and then go square dancing the next-- was not apparent to Jack.

Wrestling had given Jack command over his body, had limbered up his legs, and had loosed up his feet. He now felt free to dance, and dance he did. He danced all over the place. And before too long he memorized the calls and came to be in fair demand as a caller. He also learned other dances such as polkas, jives, and waltzes. Once he even danced on TV for Saturday Night Barn Dance Show. It was only some years later and after his first bout with cancer and a couple of minor strokes that I was able to witness his dance moves. He was still light as a feather on his feet. Right now, I just know that he is dancing before the Lord in heaven.

Jack's mother did not know about his latest passion until she came on one of her visits to Winnipeg. One evening Jack asked her if she cared to go dancing at the Legion. At first she thought that he had invited her just so that she could go dancing. She had no idea of the skill and grace he had acquired since her last visit.

It was at a square dance where Jack met and courted his first wife. By this time he was 28 and looking to settle down. She was the only young, available girl there on that particular night and so he decided to make a move. She fell for it and they got married much too quickly. The union was entered into without counseling or without much thought for the future. In fact on their wedding day the bride's mother sent a telegram stating, "Just because you married him doesn't mean you have to stay with him." She did not. Jack believed that marriage was a union for life. He did not realize that her commitment to marriage was not the same as his.

In all fairness to her, the wedding came far too soon for her to really get to know Jack. She was unaware of his learning disability and his other idiosyncrasies. She did not know what to make of a situation when he would do the exact opposite from what should be expected. He had also not told her that, due to an accident in his youth, he could never father a child. At first she made the adjustment, but later she changed her mind. Yes, she did too want to have children. It was near impossible for a marriage to survive if one had not entered into it without taking careful consideration of these factors.

It was during this time that I first met Jack. My first husband, Jack Christie (to differentiate between the two Jacks, I will call him John -- his given name), had met Jack at his wrestling events. Even before John and I were married, Jack would pick up John and take him to his matches. Once after our marriage, Jack showed up on our doorstep with his wife to present a business opportunity to us. John wasn't at home so, since I didn't know the couple, I sent them away telling them to make arrangements to return when my husband would be at home. They did, and that was the beginning of a long friendship that spanned over three decades. Once a week, Jack and his wife, and eventually just Jack, would come to our home to spend an evening playing Monopoly.

I remember the week in 1971 that the split came and Jack and his first wife's five year marriage came to an end. They came to our house as usual that week for our game night. She was on a tear. She called him down every time he opened his mouth to the extent that he finally just sat there quiet. Years later, I asked him why he had not opened his mouth to defend himself against her allegations. He simply replied, "Two wrongs don't make a right." By the time they left, I knew that they had serious problems and that their marriage was likely over.

By this time she had forced Jack to give up wrestling and they were no longer attending square dances. Life had probably become pretty dull and, considering Jack's disabilities, frustrating. But the straw that broke the camel's back is when he came home and told her he had lost his job.

One of the clubs that she held over his head was the fact that she had a bank job while he had a dead-end job, and now no job. Somehow, in her mind, that made her a better class of person than he was. If only she had known that in the not too distant future he too would be working for a bank, and with many times the responsibilities that she had on her job.

The next day she was just gone. She had taken everything that she could and left without a word of farewell. Jack was devastated. It took him over thirty years to find healing from the hurt he viewed as a betrayal; over three decades before he could trust enough to take the leap again. Only this time he had two things working for him. He would marry a woman who had known him for 35 years, who knew his problems, his weaknesses and his strengths even before entering into their union. And this time he would have the Lord's blessing on his marriage.

Chapter 7   You Can Bank On It

If Jack had known what lay ahead of him when he went to the Toronto Dominion (TD) Bank Data Centre to submit an application for a job as a night messenger he may not have had the nerve to apply. He had done shipping and receiving before, and that's what he thought this job would basically entail. It would become so much more than that.

As is often the case with new employees, when Jack was hired he was put on a three month probation. He shortly came to realize that his co-workers would be mostly women and that he would have to learn to get along with them if he wanted to pass that probationary period. This, he thought, may be a difficult proposition due to his present attitude toward all women due to his unfortunate experiences with one woman.

And the women seemed determined to make sure he didn't make it through his probation. For three months they ribbed him constantly about his single status. They wanted to know why a guy like him didn't have a woman in his life. Was he a bit different or what? He thought that if he opened his mouth to set them straight he would no longer have a job. He had to get past the three months before he could break his awful silence. I can't imagine him being quiet for so long. I know he would have loved to have teased them back. However, he felt his livelihood depended on him keeping his mouth shut; on him letting the women say what they wanted to about him without rebuttal.

But he never forgot one cutting word that they said; and he remembered who had said what. One day he confidently strode in and spoke up, "Now ladies, I will introduce you to the real Jack Ward. I will introduce you to my mind, my memory, and my sense of humor. And I remember every word that each one of you said to me about my singleness over the last three months". They looked at each other and knew that Jack's probation period had just ended. From that day on Jack Ward was one of the gang.

Jack's job was to ensure that everyone did what they were supposed to do in order to get all the posting done and the bags out by a certain time in the morning. If a computer broke down it was his job to find a solution. This was something at which he excelled. He was not really all that mechanically inclined, but he could think on his feet. Sometimes he would take parts out of one machine to make another machine capable of completing the job at hand. Somewhere, somehow he always seemed able to find the solution.

If the bags did not get out in the morning on time they would miss the messenger truck and have to be sent by some other way. Sometimes he would be that other way. In such cases he would be seen, early in the morning, scurrying down the sidewalk towards another nearby bank with a bag of postings in his hand in a hurried attempt to get his bag on their truck. If this failed a taxi would have to be hailed, thus incurring a very unwelcome expense.

Jack frequently told the story of the shift that the night manager came in drunk and fired all the computer operators. Since Jack held the key to the place, the first thing he did was to run around and lock all the doors so no one could get out. Next Jack locked all the elevators so that they could not be used. Then he locked the night manager in the vault that was being used for storage. Lastly, he called the bank manager at home and told him of the dilemma.

The bank manager told Jack to get all the people back in to work. Jack replied, "Oh, they are all here. I locked them in. And the manager is sleeping it off in the vault." Jack then went back to the girls and told them what the manager said. He told them that if they went home now they would just get called back in, so they might as well stay and finish the job. That morning all the bags went out on time as scheduled.

Jack worked the night shift for over thirteen years. Sometimes, if someone from the day shift called in sick, Jack would work a double shift. On one such occasion, after working 16 hours, he was asked to stay for a meeting concerning new fire extinguishers for the Data Centre. This was a reasonable request because at one time Jack had worked for a fire extinguisher company. However, now he was just too tired. He promptly fell asleep in the meeting. After the presentation the manager, who had seen him asleep, asked him what he thought of the presentation. Jack said that if they would go to such and such a company they could get twenty percent off. The salesman who had given the presentation quickly back peddled on his offer and stated that he would give them twenty percent off as well. Afterward, Jack's manager told him he was welcome to sleep through his meetings any time.

Jack was always a bit proud to tell the next story. One night at the beginning of his shift the bank manager approached Jack to ask him for a big favor. Apparently the employees had become interested in joining a union and had been talking to some union reps. The manager knew that Jack disliked unions and so now he was asking him to come up with some idea to abort the process before it went too far. At first he didn't have any idea what could be done, but he thought on it all night. By morning he had come up with a scheme.

He posted a note and a sign-up sheet for all the employees who would like to do a pre-Christmas curling event sponsored by the bank. There would be a free dinner and one drink for each person that would sign up and come. Now this was in addition to the company sponsored Christmas dinner that had already been held. He was asking people to sign up for a company sponsored event which he had not yet cleared with the company. Definitely a bit nervy.

Then he went home to sleep. It wasn't too long before he was awakened by the phone. At first he thought that he was going to be reprimanded, but the manager was all excited and exclaimed, "It's working. The sheet is full of names and we have had to put up more sheets." Not only did the TD Bank sponsor this event, but they went on to sponsor an annual bonspiel. And union talks came to a complete halt. Mission accomplished.

No, Jack was not your run-of-the-mill employee. He was honest to the core and was slow to back down from what he was convinced was right -- even if it might cost him his job.

The time came when the bank felt it needed to install a new security system. Jack was convinced that the new system was not as good as the system they already had. The bank manager tried to convince him to the contrary. Finally, to prove his point, Jack took an outdated credit card out of his wallet, stuck it in the slot, and walked out through the door. The manager was so angry he fired Jack on the spot.

When the manager arrived home that night he informed his wife that he had fired Jack that morning and that he would be looking for a new night messenger. His wife just looked at him and said, "We're sure going to miss you around here." Puzzled, he asked her what she meant. For an answer she reminded him of how things had been before he hired Jack, of how many nights he got called back to the bank for staffing and machine problems, and that since Jack had been hired he had been able to sleep most nights in his own bed.

The next night, believing himself to be fired, Jack did not go to work. Soon after his regular start time he received a phone call instructing him to hop a cab as soon as possible and go straight to work. Jack happily obliged.

Jack never felt the need to back down when he felt that he was in the right. He would heartily attempt to correct you, but never by personally attacking you. Likewise, he never ever felt the need to justify his actions. He was who he was, take him or leave him. If he was proven wrong he had no trouble setting things right. He was not one to harbor ill feelings or hold a grudge. When it was over, it was over and he never brought it up again. But he also refused to take abuse. He did not like the misuse of authority by anyone, and if he saw someone using their position to dish out abuse upon others, he usually tried to do something about it. One such incident bears this out.

There was a supervisor at the bank who was trying to quit smoking. Unfortunately she was suffering from severe withdrawal symptoms and as a result was making life miserable for everybody, especially the computer operators who worked under her. A complaint landed on Jack's desk informing him of the difficulties this individual was creating. However, he was not at liberty to deal with the supervisor's behavior. Nonetheless, he did not appreciate cantankerous women, so he came up with a plan whereby he would not have to approach this woman directly and yet give her the message that a complaint had been made against her. When he arrived at work and before the supervisor came in, Jack put a chair on top of her desk. He then draped his coat over the chair, put his hat at the coat collar, and his boots at the front of the chair. When the supervisor came in he jumped up on top of the desk and proceeded to scold the imaginary person in the chair telling him how his behavior was unacceptable and bad for morale, and how the women would rather he smoked than be so miserable. It had the desired effect. They all had a good laugh and the tension was over.

And so Jack became the heart of the night shift. It appeared that nothing happened unless Jack was somewhere to be seen. If Jack didn't sign up for a company sponsored event or a farewell dinner or some other such occasion, it seemed that no one else would sign up either. Sometimes the bank would even pay him to attend certain events to ensure that they were well attended.

After thirteen years of working the night shift the doctor advised Jack to stop working nights due to ill health. When a day position was not in the offering, he was forced to resign. When he left the bank for the last time, at least eight of the women also handed in their resignations. If Jack was not there to entertain them and keep them company, if he was not there to fight for them, then they would not work the night shift any longer either.

Many years later after we were married, I received a glimpse into how much he had been appreciated at the bank. We received a call that one of his fellow workers had passed away and it was

Jack's desire to attend the funeral. By now he had gone through two cancers and had changed so much in appearance that no one really recognized him during the service. It was only afterwards at the lunch that people started gravitating toward our table. One by one they came and said they did not know he was there until they heard him speak. In fact, until they heard his voice some of them did not even know he was still alive. But they all remembered that voice, and his ability to tell one story after another. Jack had a very distinctive voice. When he entered a place the volume went up and when he left it was like a whirlwind had just blown through. Many of these people had not heard that Jack had re-married. He had seemed to have gotten himself stuck in a rut. One bad marriage and years of night shift had done that to him. No one thought that he would ever climb out.

Jack always knew that he had been very fortunate and blessed to have had that bank job for over thirteen years. His learning disabilities had not seemed to have followed him there. To him, those had been his golden years. Now they were over. He drew out all his pensions from the bank and set out to try to find a new job. But he was now over fifty years old and hampered by ill health. Hundreds of resumes later he still had not found a job. His disability had once again come back to haunt him. His applications were difficult to read, and his resume appeared to be too good for what they saw of him in person. He was finally forced to give up his apartment and to move to a little trailer on the beach. By the time the resort where he had set up closed for the winter, things had really begun to look grim. His unemployment insurance had run out and he felt desolate.

Chapter 8   Cleaning Up

John, my first husband had faced the same dilemma not too long before. He finally was given the job as office cleaner for the company that employed me. We offered Jack the opportunity of joining my husband. They would acquire a few more contracts to clean other offices and thus start their own business. This was really appealing to Jack. He had often thought about going into business for himself and this was his chance.

There was one problem, however. Jack wanted to go big and my husband John was content to keep it small. Jack wanted to hand out flyers and aggressively grow the business; John, due to his own health concerns, wanted to step back and take it a bit easier. It finally got to the point where I had to tell them enough was enough. They would have to split up with my husband taking the initial contract and Jack taking the rest from which he could build his own business.

Though this ended their business relationship, it did not end our friendship. Shortly after this my husband had a massive seizure which ended his working days forever. We gave Jack the one office we had kept and he was well on his way towards making a decent income for himself.

Jack called his business "Twilight Enterprises". He worked very hard and did well. In fact, he did so well that he opened a second branch called "Senior's Sunshine". For this he hired women who traveled from place to place cleaning houses and apartments for seniors.

At first this branch did very well. Jack offered his clients a good rate from which he paid his employees, supply costs and advertizing expenses, plus a little for himself. But then costs went up. In spite of rising input costs, Jack could not bring himself to ask for more money from his seniors. As previously mentioned, finances were never Jack's strong suit. He undercut other companies to get work, but as a result he did not make much money for all of his time, effort and expense.

It was after he had started "Senior's Sunshine" that Jack wrote his first Christmas letter. He empathized with the seniors who had no one to visit them and, apparently, had no one who cared about them. He began to care more about them than he cared about his income. He just wanted to cheer up his older clients, as well as the many others that he began to add to his mailing list.

These letters proved to be quite costly. At first he had them professionally printed from his handwritten draft. I don't know how the printers were able to decipher his handwriting, but they did -- most of the time. After a few years he asked me if I could do it for him. This was long before we were anything more than family friends. I agreed because I realized that the letters were more expensive than what he could really afford. He usually mailed out more than one hundred copies each year.

There is a Christmas story that Jack loved to

tell. He said that it was the favorite of all his cleaning stories. It took place on a blizzardy Christmas Eve. An elderly lady phoned to ask him if he could come and clean her residence. Jack had asked one of the women on his team to stand by just in case a last minute call came in. Because of the severe weather he decided to chauffeur the cleaning lady to the job and help carry in the equipment. When they arrived, they found that the snow was so bad that they could not get close to the client's building. Then they realized that the client lived on the top floor of a two and a half story house. Jack jokingly called it "the penthouse suite".

When they arrived at the client's door she was surprised that they had come in such inclement weather, and then offered them a cup of tea. They gladly accepted. The lady stepped out on her little balcony and took a single, previously used, teabag from off the clothes line to make tea for the two of them. Jack excused himself, walked to the corner store, bought her a box of one hundred teabags, and never charged her for the cleaning.

Jack loved Christmas. This was evident when you saw how he decorated the house he rented in his old neighborhood of Brooklyn. He had toy villages and nativity scenes, both lit and unlit, everywhere in the house.

These were lonely years for Jack. He could easily identify with his seniors and anyone else who lived alone with no family around to care about them. Our family usually invited him over for dinner either on Christmas Eve or Christmas day, but the rest of the time he was alone. He would always wrap one present for himself to put under his own tree so that he would have something to open on Christmas morning.

It was only years later that I realized that he had always presented himself with a gift to place under the tree so that he would have something to open on Christmas morning. We would give him a gift when he came over, but we always wanted him to open it at our house. We never thought about giving him one to open at his own home on Christmas morning. I now wonder why we never picked up on this. I guess he was not given to complaining.

I wonder why we did not invite him to stay overnight when he came to dinner on Christmas Eve and played Santa to our girls. That way he could have awakened on Christmas morning with a family around him. Somehow when you have family, you tend to forget about the one person in whose life you could really make a difference. After his first wife left him, he spent over thirty years getting up alone at Christmas. What a shame when I think of it now.

It was only after we were married that I came to realize how lonely his Christmases and other holidays had been. I slowly began to understand why he so enjoyed Christmas and why he had a tendency to go overboard on decorations. He was so aware of the importance of happy memories at

Christmas. This is why, when he later spent Christmas in palliative care at the Portage District Hospital, he was determined not to die during the Christmas season -- he did not want me to have this as a memory in all my Christmases to come. He did not want to spoil this season of celebration for me or for my family. He wanted us to always treasure the holidays without sad memories.

Jack had no family left that he knew of. My family became his family. For those years my immediate family, my husband and two children, were his family. Later, when we were married, he embraced my siblings and their families as family. He was always grateful for the family he came to call his own. And this of course included our church family. He loved them dearly, and in his prayers he never forgot to pray for them. Nor did he forget our friends and neighbors. They were all precious to him.

Chapter 9 The Storyteller

Jack's early life was full of adventure and fun. It seems that he had more stories to tell than the average boy. Maybe this was because he had such a keen memory and everything he ever did seemed to be etched in his mind for life. In school he was called slow, but his friends saw what a genius he was. When there was a funny poem or line to be remembered, they went to Jack. When they needed funny words set to a certain song, again Jack was called upon.

Jack was a prolific storyteller. He loved to tell stories. Many of these were true, but sometimes he was given to exaggeration. Some were funny, and some were sad, but mostly he liked to make people laugh. If he had a true story that would make people laugh he would tell it. If he didn't he would tell jokes. Jack honestly believed that his mission in life was to make people laugh. He had the gift of telling stories so that even the most uninteresting event could become laughable when turned over in his mind. Even his hospital bed became a platform for him to tell stories. I believe God directed people into his room just to cheer them up.

Jack never had a problem finding something to say, either as a comeback to someone else's comment, to tease someone, or to defend himself from some sort of trouble he had gotten himself into. I think he was born with a quick tongue. His mother once caught him running out the door without closing it, again. She called after him, "Were you born in a barn?" His quick response was, "If it was good enough for Jesus, it's good enough for me." Instead of calling him back she closed the door for him. Jack turned around just long enough to see his mother having a good laugh over his quick response.

One thing that he could never stand was a lull in the conversation. In such cases he would always jump in to fill the silence with a joke or a story. Also, I noticed that if the topic being discussed was one that he knew nothing or very little about, he would wait until there was a pause in the conversation and then he would quickly tell a story or change the topic to one with which he was more familiar. I think that he wanted to let people know that he was still there and could not be ignored. This behavior was not always understood by some.

There are a number of true stories that he specified that he would like me to tell in his book.

One day Jack and his school buddy Art Cheadle decided to take a hand-pumped railway jigger for a ride. Often these ideas were Jack's, and this time was no exception. As they neared the village of Rosser, about 25 kilometers up the track, they noticed a train approaching. The jigger was a heavy thing to come off the track and so the two young boys heaved and strained until, just in time, they got it off the rails. As the train approached they realized that it was on a different track. After it had passed, they determined that there was no way they could get the jigger back on to the rails. They would have to walk home, but not along the railroad right-of-way lest they be seen by the authorities. And so they followed the winding course of Sturgeon Creek the long way back. When their parents questioned them why they were so late getting home they simply replied that they had been out walking and lost track of time.

Jack never told his father about this adventure. William was employed by the railroad, and he would never have approved of his son utilizing railway property in this manner.

There were other things that Jack never told his father, like hanging on to the back bumper of a car and sliding down a snow-covered street or hitching a ride on a moving railway car. On another occasion Jack and his buddies decided that it would be fun to ride to school on the caboose of a passing train. They decided that they would jump off before they got too near the school so that they wouldn't get caught. When it came time to jump all of the other boys bailed on the side opposite the school building. Jack, however, was dyslexic and often confused his right from his left. When all of his buddies went one way, he went the other -- and landed right on the hood of the principal's car. Not good at all!

Jack's parents used to go to Winnipeg Beach by train on Saturdays in the summer. On occasion Jack's friend Art would come along. One such day they had a swim and then went into the men's change room to get into their street clothes. While changing they saw some poetry written on the wall that intrigued their young minds. On the way home Art mentioned the poems and stated that it was too bad they didn't have something on which they could have written them down. Jack asked him which one he wanted to know and proceeded to quote them all from memory word for word. Both Art and Jack's father were thoroughly amazed at this. In such a short time Jack had memorized those poems so that he could write them down when he got home.

Jack always worked hard to get around his learning disability. One of the ways he had discovered to retain things was to memorize them. Thus he developed a system to memorize that allowed him to remember things that others could not. He often memorized special lines in songs he heard with the intention of turning them to suit his purpose at some future time. His memory was truly his best tool and he used it in every aspect of life.

Once in a while Jack would tell the story about something that had made him very happy. After he and Art had joined the boy scouts they became aware that their scout leader and his wife had a new baby daughter. It was just a few weeks until Christmas, and the boys decided that they would like to buy a gift for this little girl. As they were walking and talking, contemplating what they should do, they came face to face with a beautiful doll in a store window.

Now there was a bit of a problem. Due to many little offences that they had committed, they had been banned from entering most of the stores in their neighborhood. But they really wanted that doll. They would need to apologize for their previous behavior. So they gathered up their courage and entered the store. The store owner accepted their apology, but there was a catch to purchasing this particular doll. The price tag was $10.00, but since this doll was put out by the Coca-Cola bottling company they were informed that they also needed to collect one hundred bottle caps. There was no way they could drink that much pop in such a short time. That meant that they needed the store owner's cooperation to save enough caps. And because time was so short, not only this store, but help from all of the stores in the area. They decided to do the hard thing and apologize in all of the stores from which they had been banished. The end result was that, not only did they get the doll for their scout leader's daughter by Christmas, but more importantly they had made their wrongs right and once again had a clean slate with all the store owners in their area.

One summer day Jack and Art were strolling down the sidewalk in their scout uniforms. As they walked past a young couple's house a young woman came running out of the house with a young child in her arms crying for help. The baby was choking and she didn't know what to do. Jack grabbed the child, handed it to Art, and gave the child one quick whack across the back. The baby started to cry and then to breathe again. Jack said he never heard anything more about it so he assumed that all was well. He never made too much of the situation. It was just a quick reflex action to an obvious need. He said he just had to try something and that he really couldn't make things worse than what they already were.

Another occasion didn't end quite as well. The boys had been going to Scouts and had learned how to tie a bowline to aid in rescuing people. It was described as a safe knot to use for that purpose. Apparently they decided to try practicing this knot at recess time. Jack had tied his friend to a tree with a bowline knot and then, for some reason, forgot to let him loose when the bell rang signaling the end of recess. When Art did not show up for class, Jack had to tell the teacher that he forgot to let him out of the tree. This little trick brought the police to the school and both mothers to the principal's office. At first it looked bad for Jack until the boys explained what kind of knot had been tied, what it was used for, and how they had come to practice it in the school yard. The mothers had a good laugh and the boys got off with a good scolding.

That Jack was an instigator in much of the high jinks that landed them in hot water is demonstrated by the next story that he told me. On one occasion the boys received permission after school to build a bit of a blaze in their backyard fire pit in order to roast some potatoes. This was fine, but what they really wanted was fresh garden potatoes and they had none of their own. The neighbor had lots, but they were already in hot water with him. One couldn't just go and pull up a potato plant. That would not be acceptable at all. Jack told his friends that the thing to do was to stay on this side of the fence and dig underneath it into the adjacent row of potatoes. In this way they could take the odd potato from various plants along the row. The plant would still be there and they would not be discovered. This worked out fine for them and they never did get caught.

Not only did Jack love to tell stories, but he was such a character that people also loved to tell stories on him.

Jack used to say, "I can get into trouble just being me". He was quite right. During Jack's square dancing days there was a gathering of like feet in a home in Carman, Manitoba. There was a powder room with two entrances in the house and Jack, not knowing that a woman had entered from the kitchen, entered a few minutes later from the unlocked door in the hallway. He found himself face to face with this woman. They, of course, were both quite shocked to find themselves in the same powder room at the same time. Merle, the lady of the house, told us that this had never happened before, so we knew that if it would happen to anyone, it would, of course, happen to Jack.

Our friend Debra Hummel has a couple stories that she likes to relate about Jack. Jack and Debra first met at a first aid course put on by the TD Bank. They were both employed by the bank but worked in different departments, Jack in the Data Centre and Debra as a teller. Through the course they became fairly good friends. One July day Debra decided she needed to go car shopping. She had been told to always take a man with you when you go looking for a car, so she decided to ask her new friend. At the time Debra was driving a VW with a heater that would not shut off. This may have been fine in winter but it wasn't so great in July. Though Jack consented to go along, he was not comfortable enough in their relationship to inform her of his discomfort caused by the malfunctioning heater. He kept quiet until he just couldn't take the heat anymore. Finally he said to her, "When I am done on this side, would you please turn me over?"

At another time Debra was in the ladies section of a large department store looking for an intimate garment. All of a sudden she heard this booming voice calling out, "Lady, can I help you with that underwear?" She commented that she had never known anyone like Jack. He could embarrass you to tears and yet he was the kindest person she had ever met.

Debra also stated that Jack loved one-liners. Once when his co-workers pressured him to bring a date to a bank sponsored event his comment had been, "I'll go to the cemetery and see if I can dig up a warm one".

Jack was strong on friendships. Most he kept for years, if not for life. One such friend was Nora Stewart. She knew Jack since he was fourteen. They kept in contact throughout the years and, when it came to the end, she visited him in palliative care and then one last time to say good-bye at his memorial service. She stated that there were many funny things that Jack did as a young man, but that he was mainly just a good and loyal friend. Though she couldn't think of a specific story to tell, she said that she did remember that she and Jack had spent much time talking to each other. They really did seem to understand each other and she has told me more than once how pleased she was that Jack had finally married me. She did tell me how Jack and her sister used to torment each other. Once he mercilessly teased her until she turned and threw a whole dishpan of dirty water on him. Then the chase was on. According to Jack, he chased her all the way across a field. However, she was faster than he was and so outran him. Jack used to think she wore too much eye make-up, so he always called her "the girl with eyes". Every Christmas Jack always insisted on hand delivering his Christmas letter to Nora and each year there was always an extra one to give to "the girl with eyes".

Alva Cowan was another old friend of Jack's who had many stories to tell. They were each other's social event nearly every morning. For the last number of years Jack and Alva talked on the phone for an hour or more each day. Correction. Jack talked for more than an hour each day. Alva listened. Sometimes Alva would have something that he needed to tell us and so he would interrupt Jack just long enough to tell Jack that he needed to talk with me for a minute. While Alva relayed his message to me, Jack would go into the back room and continue the conversation all by himself. Just a short time ago Alva told me how much he misses those long talks.

Jack and Alva actually met while they were square dancing and they never lost touch. In fact, it was Jack who introduced Alva to June, the woman Alva would later marry. Jack had met June at Toastmasters and had taken her out a few times. After a while, Jack introduced Alva to June as she was closer in age to Alva than she was to him. After Alva and June were married, Jack continued, with Alva's blessing, to take June to Toastmasters.

Jack and June had much in common. They

both loved sports. In fact, I think she loved sports even more than Jack did. After Jack and I were married, I would hear him talking on the phone and think it was Alva. Then I would discover that it was he and June talking sports. These two old friends were engrossed in conversation, and all was well in the world.

One year Alva and June gave Jack a Christmas present on Boxing Day, the 26th of December. When Jack opened the present and saw a new Christmas lights box he decided to just put the box away until the next Christmas. Alva waited a few days and then couldn't stand it any longer. He called to see how Jack had enjoyed his gift. Jack said, "Very well. Thank you. I will put them up next Christmas." Alva then queried, "You never looked in the box, did you?" The box did not contain Christmas lights as Jack had thought. A few weeks before Jack had helped Alva put up new lights at his place. That was the origin of the box. Finally, when he actually opened his present he discovered a full box of duct tape.

This was great. Jack was very fond of duct tape. In shades of "Red Green", the TV persona created by Steve Smith, he fixed everything with duct tape. Before we were married, I even found some of his socks where he had mended the holes with that stuff. A friend had once asked him if he wanted a new pair of slippers for Christmas or should she just get him a new roll of duct tape.

Alva and June knew just what he would do with this tape. At the time Jack had an old Dodge Ram truck that he used to haul equipment he needed for his job. The truck was the same silver gray as the duct tape, and it had a fender that was beginning to be compromised with rust. There was just enough tape to hold that old truck together for a little while longer.

Jack's friend Al Hammerton shared a memory with me at our wedding. Apparently he, Jack, and a few other fellows were away at a square dancing event and were staying at a hotel on the American side of the border. Jack was sporting quite a moustache at the time, and the guys had decided that it was time that it should come off. Of course, Jack was well rehearsed in the discipline of wrestling and so was nigh unto impossible to pin down. Not to be dissuaded, they managed to entice him to an open window to supposedly look at something of interest. When he stuck his head and shoulders through the window to see what they were trying to show him, they closed the window on him as hard as they dared to prevent his escape. With him thus incapacitated they proceeded to cut off half his moustache. Once one half of his moustache was gone he gladly cut off the other half.

There is one more story that I have to tell that actually involved me long before we were married. I was doing some volunteer driving for

Child and Family Services and had taken some children to St. Laurant, Manitoba after they had been on a family visit in Winnipeg. When I was about to leave, I discovered that my car would not start. The timing belt had broken and now I needed to find a way to get it back to the city. It would have been quite expensive to call a tow truck, so I called Jack instead. We had been friends for long enough that I felt that this was not too much to ask of him. He showed up in that old Dodge Ram truck. There was really nothing wrong with that; a good sized vehicle for towing was perfect. However, instead of bringing a chain with which to pull me, he brought a rope that kept on breaking. After several such breakages, he stopped at a service station and acquired a short chain. This should certainly hold. It did.

About half way home it started to rain and the temperature began dropping. Because the car was not running I had no heat in the car. Soon the windows fogged up and I had to open the driver's window in an attempt to see out.

Jack was normally a very sensitive man. He often cried when others sorrowed. But sometimes he did not know how to reason things through. When the weather turned cold his mind shifted gears. His one thought became his need to get Miranda home before she freezes back there with the window open and no gloves. How would he accomplish this? To him the obvious answer was to drive faster and so arrive home sooner. It did not occur to him what would happen to a driver whose vision was hampered while being hooked to another vehicle that was going faster than could be managed. He also failed to realize that I had no power steering and no power brakes. I panicked and more than once attempted to brake, but nothing much happened. I flashed my lights. He didn't know what I wanted but thought I must be getting colder and so he needed to speed up. He was already towing me at 100 km/h. I thought I was having a nervous breakdown. When we got to the garage and unhooked my car, I couldn't even tell him what was wrong. I just collapsed in tears. I couldn't even speak. Fear and cold had got my tongue. And he couldn't understand why I was being so emotional.

He took me home, and then he went to talk to a mechanic friend of his. He told him about the cold and the speed of the drive, and then he asked him what he could have possibly done wrong. His friend told him he was crazy. He said he should never have gone over 50 km/h. He further stated that if that would have been him, he would have jumped out of the vehicle at the first corner and let Jack take the car home by himself. It would have been far safer to walk home for hours alone on the highway.

Jack was honest to the core. He came back to tell me he had worked it out and he now knew why I had panicked. He still maintained, however, that he only had my well being in mind. He had nearly killed me with his kind intentions. I really had to make a choice to forgive him for that one.

Chapter 10 The "C" Word

The time came when Jack's business began to slow down, because Jack was slowing down. He was slowly losing steam. At first no one noticed except that he had been losing a little bit of weight each year. After my first husband passed away in 1994, I started to help him with some jobs in the evening. I needed to fill the hours that I used to go to visit my husband in a personal care home, and Jack seemed to be needing help more often.

By 2001 he was starting to turn jobs away. He did not look good. I finally convinced him to move out of his apartment and to move into the seniors' complex where I lived. It was easier for me to go to another floor to check up on him than it was to drive half way across the city to see how he was doing.

That move was an awful experience for both of us. There was stuff that had to be discarded, but every time I put something in the garbage, his crazy neighbor, who was buying the house, would retrieve it for herself and move it back in. It just seemed like a totally useless exercise. Why was I even making the effort?

On the day of the move, Jack did a cleaning job in the morning while another lady and I were at his house attempting to finish packing. I had already been there every evening after work for a week and now I was spent. As the day progressed I began suffering from stress related chest pains. I ended up in the hospital and my moving day was over. When the doctor discovered what I had been up to, he made sure that I wasn't discharged until the move was done. That didn't help Jack. He was sick too, and now guilt was added to his load. Finally enough people rallied around him with trucks and things and they got him moved. When I came home I had never seen Jack look so bad. He was still upbeat, but he looked very sick.

In October of that year he closed most of his business. He kept one office cleaning job until he was admitted to the hospital on December 20th.

In November we went to a church Christmas dinner together and an old lady got up and gave Jack her chair when he walked in the door. He looked like death warmed over. His skin had started yellowing, and he could not eat much. He had been going to the doctor at least once a week but they hadn't discovered anything yet.

On December 19th he was sitting in my living room when he decided that he wanted something from the store. I offered to go get it for him, but he refused. He went out, ran for the bus, and as soon as he entered the bus he collapsed on the floor. He was only out for a short time before he roused. Later we ascertained that it was at that moment that a blood clot that had been in his leg for some time broke loose and lodged in his lung. He got up, did his shopping, and then took the same bus home. The bus driver had wanted to call an ambulance on his ride to the store. Now, seeing the pain on Jack's face, he again wanted to call for help. Jack refused and so the call went unmade.

By the next morning, December 20th, his pain had become unbearable. After much coaxing, he allowed his friend Alva to take him to Grace Hospital where he would remain for many days. The first thing the doctors had to deal with was the blood clot, but there obviously were more problems. The color of his skin and the sores on his arms and legs indicated that he had liver problems. Once all the tests were run and the results in, it was determined that he had non-Hodgkin's lymphoma. And it was in the final stage. The cancer specialist informed me that they would try chemo, but not to hold my breath. She had never before seen this disease progress to this stage without being diagnosed.

This locket is apparent proof that Jack was not adopted. Jack as a toddler is pictured on the right with a portrait of his father on the left.

Jack as a toddler   Jack at age 5

Top Left: Jack
with Lucille and
William at
Winnipeg Beach
Bottom Left:
Lucille and Jack
with paternal
grandmother who
was on a year-
long visit from
England.
Bottom Right:
Jack and grand-
mother with bike
decorated for
community
parade.

Top: "Christmas Jack" 1956
Bottom: William Ward, Art
Cheadle, and Jack
1958

Top: Jack in about 1953
Bottom: Jack with
Laddie in 1954

Jack "Killer" Ward
Age 19   1957

Art Cheadle and Jack present
"Best Sport of the Year to
Dominic Duao ca. 1966

Square Dancing
Jack in fringed shirt

Jack and Square Dancing
Partner - 1964

Top Left:
ca. 1976

Top Right:
1984

Bottom Left:
Wedding 2003

Bottom Right:
Jack with Baby
2012

Friends
through
thick and
thin.
Jack with
Miranda
Christie
Christmas
2002

Mr. & Mrs. Jack Ward - 2003

Christmas 2010

Jack with Henry Carlson 2011

Jack with John Searcy - 2012

Terry Fox Run 2012

These next pictures demonstrate Jack's unique sense of humour:

Farmers in the Dell
2007

In the doghouse
2008

Skateboarding with Baby - 2007

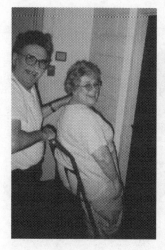

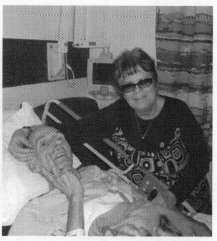

Crossing the
Threshold 2003

Crossing the Threshold
2014

Ward/Christie family - Christmas 2013

Chapter 11 Something Worth Living For

It was now New Year's Eve and everyone was busy. However, Pastor Bob, my minister from Ness Avenue Baptist Church, was a compassionate man and took the time out of his schedule to go and see Jack. He had visited with him before, but this day was different. Jack had been told he might not ever go home again and Pastor Bob agreed that he had never seen anybody look this bad and survive. Pastor Bob wanted to know if Jack thought he had everything in his life in order. Was he ready to die? And if he died, where was he planning to end up? Jack wasn't really sure he could answer that question. He told the pastor that he thought he would be okay because he had always tried to be the best he could.

We were sitting in a lounge area with a big open window. There were no pencil sharpeners, but there was a window. Pastor Bob drew a diagram of two hillsides with a large chasm between. He drew Jack on one hill and God on the other. Then he pointed out to him that in order to get to heaven he had to get from his hill to God's hill and asked him how he could do that. Jack wasn't too sure, but he figured that he would need some kind of a key.

Then Pastor Bob drew in a cross that spanned the chasm and told Jack that this was the key. Only the finished work of Christ on the cross could save us from eternal death. Jack saw for the first time that all of the good works that he thought he had done for all his seniors and many others would not get him there. He needed the sinless Jesus to die for him so he did not have to die for his own sin. While sitting there and looking out the large window he finally realized that God loved him enough to send His Son to die for him. I still have that drawing. I could not shred it with all of the other miscellaneous papers. It was a part of the tapestry of his life. I had talked to him about these things before, but he just couldn't comprehend them. I wish I had known earlier about his pencil sharpener story.

In the late afternoon of that New Year's Eve Jack became a new person. For him old things had passed away and all things had become new. The new year signaled new life.

Jack's working days were over. I was his Power of Attorney, so it was my job to close down the rest of his business, to collect any outstanding bills, and to proceed to clean out his apartment. If he were to die, there would be no money to continue paying his rent. His bank was very cooperative and helped all they could, but many of the things that required doing were labor intensive and time consuming.

We had no sooner heard Jack's diagnosis when I received word that my 85 year old mother was dying of Parkinson's in a Steinbach personal care home. I was still working at this time, but I decided to take early retirement so that I could travel back and forth between Jack and my mom.

We did not know who would go first. Both were grim.

In early January 2002 they decided to give Jack his first chemo treatment. He nearly died. By now he weighed only 130 pounds and was not really strong enough to benefit from chemo. They decided against continuing with the treatment. They gave him three weeks to two months to live. But Jack was determined to live and felt they should keep on trying. We had a meeting with the doctors to determine if he should have more chemo or just be admitted into palliative care. Jack chose two more treatments. The doctors' response was that it would kill him. Jack replied that that was okay. He said if I don't try I'll never know if it could have worked. He knew that with the chemo he had a small chance to survive; without it he had no chance at all. Besides, now he knew where he was going when he died, so everything would be alright either way. He did agree to go into palliative care if the chemo was not successful. I didn't believe he would live long enough to get there.

Jack was now confident that God was on his side and he made God a promise. He told Him that if He brought him through this he would do two things. First off, he would ask me to marry him, and then he would trust and serve the God of these miracles for the rest of his life. We had talked about marriage before, but I had told him that it would not happen unless we were of the same faith.

Before Jack could receive his second chemo

he needed to undergo nine hours of blood transfusions. The next day, before the chemo was administered, Pastor Jeff, a minister from the church my brother Cliff attended, came to pray over Jack during his treatment. Something happened. God's healing seemed evident.

That chemo went very well. His white blood cell count went too low, but they had meds ready for that. He never even got sick. He did, however, have to spend the rest of the time he was in the hospital in isolation. Due to his low white blood cell count, it was feared that if he would pick up some bug he would not have the strength to combat it. He had his second treatment three weeks later. He just kept improving after that.

In March I received a call from the hospital. I was informed that Jack could go home that afternoon. I was taken a bit by surprise. And I was on the horns of a dilemma. I had never expected Jack to ever leave the hospital. As his Power of Attorney I had given his landlord a month notice on his suite and had disposed of many of his things. He did not even have a bed anymore.

Unfortunately, I had also gotten rid of much of Jack's writings up to this point. I had picked out a few choice selections that I felt would be sentimental to him if he ever did come home. There was also some other of his possessions that I kept just in case this happened. Upon letting his apartment go, I argued with myself and finally concluded that I could store some of his more precious things in my small suite until we knew where all this would end. This turned out to be a very good choice. However, I did make some errors in judgment by keeping some items he didn't really care about and by discarding some things he actually did care about. But what was done was done. I could not undo it, so we both had to live with some regret; me with remorse over the pain I caused him, and Jack with sorrow over that which was forever lost. I will ever be grateful that he forgave me for my miscalculations as to what was valuable to him.

In some ways, removing all this clutter was a good thing, a sort of cleansing. Jack had decided to live life anew and a lot of the things that I discarded were just so much baggage that he was better off without. The book that would have been written from that material would have had a much different tone. His life in Christ was much different than the life he lived before. He had become what God wanted him to become and his old life was not one to commemorate in all its detail.

The hospital agreed to keep him one more day so that Home Care could bring him a bed and a wheel chair. The palliative care people at the hospital loaned him a walker for six months. I noted that everything that he was given had a six month loan period on them. I got brave and asked the nurse about this. After beating around the bush for awhile she finally admitted that Jack's prognosis was only for a six months survival.

I was not pleased with the news, but what could I do? He was still here, and six months was better than the two months they had previously given him. Since the landlord had not re-rented Jack's apartment yet, I went and paid the next month's rent and Jack moved back in.

Jack came home in March 2002, 77 days after being admitted into the hospital on that December morning. What a celebration we had that evening. It was very quiet, but extremely joyful. We praised God for such a miracle. By now we were quite sure that God was doing something special in Jack's life. He had gone from gravely ill to the remote possibility of a remission in those days in the hospital. The combination of the right chemo drugs coupled with many prayers seemed to be working better than was originally anticipated, even by his doctor.

There were still some obvious problems. The blood clot, the original reason why he had agreed to seek medical help, had been cleared up. However, while in the hospital he had suffered two strokes that had gone untreated. He had been too sick for them to be concerned about that. As a result, he could not lift the toes on his right foot when the foot was planted on the floor. When walking, his toes would drag and snag. It was because of this that he needed the walker. He did not really need the wheelchair. His walker had wheels and a good seat. If we were walking and he became tired he could sit down and I could wheel him the rest of the way to his suite.

Jack came home with no hair. He was okay with that. But he also came home with absolutely no voice, not even a whisper. That he did mind. He lived in his suite by himself and if anyone phoned him he could not talk loud enough to be heard. Then they would call me concerned whether or not he was alright. We took him to a specialist to see why he could not talk and they said it was just the chemo. Like his hair, it should come back in time.

Another thing he was missing was his memory. He had always had a great memory. But now he had forgotten all of his old jokes and he was unable to tell any of his stories. He could just barely remember his name. The cancer specialist was quite concerned about this. It could mean that the cancer had gone to his brain. However, she felt that the chemo had taken too much out of him to submit him to any more testing.

In May that year we celebrated Jack's 64th birthday. This was a major event. We had been told he would not live more than two months. It was now five months later. We had a party in my suite and invited as many guests as we could get in.

Jack had five more chemo treatments after leaving the hospital. He had his last one in September of 2002. About a month later he came up to my place to watch some TV. As he was sitting there I witnessed something that I had never seen in any other person before. Jack's eyes had been dead for months. There was very little expression in

77

them. There was only a deep sadness, a sense of loss in the knowledge that life could have been so much different. This was true not only for him personally, but also for us had we not waited so long to decide to spend the rest of our lives together. I had never seen dead eyes come to life before, but that is just how it seemed to me.

As he was sitting there I saw a faint smile creep across his face. Then a big grin. And finally he just burst out laughing. This all happened over a very short period of time. And it was happening right in front of my eyes. I looked in his eyes and realized that a light had just been switched on. I asked him what was so funny. He chortled that he had just remembered one of his old jokes.

A few days later we had an appointment with the cancer specialist. She asked me if there was anything new. I told her what I had seen and she smiled. This was exactly what she had been waiting for. After seeing the results of his CT scan she declared that his lymphoma was in remission for now. We sent his hospital bed and wheelchair back to Home Care and he put the walker aside. It was time to get on with life.

Jack's illness and his commitment to God had changed his life forever. He was a new man. He was not the man I had previously known. He was still crazy, and funny, and kind, but he had a new purpose in life. His new life meant that he needed to learn again. I wondered how he could do this. I still don't quite understand how he managed to learn all he did after his life changing decision, but I do know he did learn. And he used what he learned to make life more fulfilling both for himself, for me, and for many others.

Now that there was a promise of some longevity, it was time for Jack to re-evaluate his life. He had made some promises to God based upon God sparing him. One day he came up to my place and asked me what I thought God would want from him now that he was going to live a little while longer. I told him that I could not answer that for him. I stated that he needed to find that out from God for himself. To do that, he would have to consider his original promises to God and begin by fulfilling them one promise at a time.

Chapter 12 Walking the Aisle

Jack had his last treatment in September of 2002. On Christmas Day he popped the big question that he had been avoiding for over thirty years. It took him that long to overcome the hurt and fear that came with the breakup of his first marriage. God had not only healed his body, but He had also healed his heart. On that Christmas morning he presented me with an engagement ring. A June wedding was planned. Thus he had kept his first promise to God.

The second promise involved getting to know God better and to find out what He wanted from him. One day he asked me what I thought about the fact that God had spared him from death. I told him that if God spared him, He had a plan for him. I told him that it was up to him to figure out exactly what that was and that it might take him some time to do so. This was especially true because of his learning disabilities. He did not possess much Bible knowledge and, with his inability to read well, I knew that this would take a considerable period of time to rectify. One thing that Jack had going for him though was integrity. He was honest and when he said he was going to make his life count for something for God, he meant it. He would never back down on such a promise to God.

Life got very busy after this. Not only did I have my own wedding plans to make, but my youngest daughter Twyla was getting married two weeks before Jack and I. We had showers for both prospective brides, varied outings with friends, all added to the regular busyness of life. In the midst of all this commotion we failed to assess the importance of what seemed to be a minor problem. Jack still had a persistent sore near his rectum that the doctors said was a bedsore left from his stay in the hospital. He would mention it to the doctor and she would take a look at it and then give him another cream. This continued into our marriage and would become an ongoing source of anguish.

June 8, 2003, the day of our wedding came. One of our guests described it had as the funniest and the "funnest" wedding he had ever attended. This was due in part to the fact that if Jack had a humorous thought in his head it would never stay there for very long. By long experience, I knew that if something triggered such a thought, a witty comment was sure to follow -- even if it was in the middle of the ceremony. I had to be prepared for this. and it was a good thing that I was. At one point in the service the pastor asked Jack if we had to get married because I had gotten rid of all his things while he was in the hospital. He responded, "No, we have to get married because if we don't she will kill me with a two-by-four. I know that Jack thought nothing of blurting out such a comment, and that he assumed that everyone would know what he meant. The statement produced much laughter, but I believe that I was the only other person who knew what he was talking about. To this day I have never explained to the pastor or anyone else in attendance what Jack meant. Now I will.

Years before, while we were still just friends, we had gone to Little Mountain Park in northwest Winnipeg for a picnic. Jack had decided in a rare moment to bring steak along to BBQ. Long before it was cooked well enough for me, he wanted to test a small piece. It was very hot, and while attempting to cool it in his mouth, he inhaled it into his windpipe. The next thing I know, I see him jumping up and down and changing colors. I was not tall enough nor my arms long enough to get them around his chest way up there in order to do the "Heimlich maneuver". Then I spotted a short piece of two-by-four lumber lying on the ground. I threw him over the picnic table, picked up the two-by-four and used it to compress his chest to dislodge the piece of steak. It worked. I probably saved his life, but he forever after made fun of me by saying that I had attacked him and tried to kill him with a two-by-four.

I doubt if anyone in the congregation understood this exchange, and I may never know what they thought of me. Hopefully they were aware of Jack's way of wording things. But it's okay. Everyone knew we were happy.

When we left the church that day, life didn't take on a rose-colored hue. Probably the main reason for this was Jack's "bed sore" that refused to heal. It wasn't until the night after the ceremony that I realized just how bad this sore was. I knew something was bugging him at the wedding. He did not even sit down to eat. He stayed on his feet and wandered around talking to people. I thought he was doing it just being sociable. What he was really doing was trying hard to be comfortable enough to stay at his own wedding meal.

Jack was determined to be a good husband. He had had one failed marriage and he knew that hadn't solely been because of his ex-wife's failures. He realized that he too had made more than his fair share of mistakes, and he was determined not to repeat them again. He knew that he was the same person with the same disabilities so that now he would have to try twice as hard. But how do you do this when you are in constant pain? He was miserable and for good reason. Due to his discomfort, we were often prevented from going places and doing things. We couldn't go on a honeymoon because that involved travel and Jack couldn't sit for long because of the burning pain. We would miss church and family functions and some thought that he was trying to keep me away from my friends and family. Nothing was farther from the truth.

It took over a year and a half after we were married for Jack's "bed sore" to be properly diagnosed. It took nine doctors that long to decide to do a biopsy, even though two of them had requested that it be taken earlier. However, another doctor would look at it and say something like, "It looks like it is healing" or "We should do a colonoscopy" or something else other than the performing the biopsy that had been requested. Some of the doctors had seen him several times and would always just prescribe another cream. Finally, one doctor pushed to have the biopsy done and the result came back as rectal cancer. At last, a diagnosis that made sense! He was given twenty radiation treatments and it was cleared up in January of 2005, nearly three years after he had been released from the hospital. The whole process had really gotten to us, and it was a particularly difficult way to start our marriage. The doctor told us at this time that this would not be the last time that we saw this cancer. His words would prove to be all too true.

When Jack was most miserable, his learning disabilities would become more pronounced. He just would not have the physical and mental strength to compensate for them. Sometimes I thought about trying to get him to take some medication to help him through. I never pushed it though, because I feared that the drugs would interfere with his spontaneous nature. I had fallen in love with his spontaneity, his ability to solve problems, and his desire to make people laugh. I did not want to see him lose that again.

Shortly after this, Jack started to have another problem. He started to have some kind of spells that were later concluded to be mild seizures. This scared me half to death. John, my first husband had very much the same kind of seizures and ended up in a care facility for the last 6 ½ years of his life. Jack's symptoms during the seizures and his behaviors afterwards were nearly identical to those of John's. Did I have to go through this again?

During a medical appointment the doctor informed us that these seizures could easily be remedied with medication. John had undergone 288 shock treatments to address his malady. I believe that these contributed to his death. Now I was being told that he could have been given a little pill to resolve his condition. I decided that day to be more proactive in the health choices that we were offered. I would be more informed about the medical conditions diagnosed and more educated as to what could be done to treat them.

Chapter 13 Life with Jack

Jack was an incredible tease. If Jack teased you that pretty well meant that you were okay in his books. He teased my granddaughter Carrie, he teased my cousin Lillian, and he mercilessly teased the caretakers in our seniors' building where we lived. For several years we had a caretaker named Ruth. She lived in the building with her twin sister Susan, who was not well. It, therefore, fell to Ruth to do most of the work. Jack loved to tease and torment Ruth every which way but up. He used to wait for her when it was her day to clean our hallway. Sometimes she would try to delay it a bit thinking that he would forget or give up and that she could then whip through the hall in a hurry before he discovered her. Soon she found out that this didn't work. He would simply pull up a chair from inside our suite and sit there and wait for her. The elevator door would open and there he sat, right in front of our door which was located next to the elevator. She would just throw her arms in the air and give up. There was no getting around him. They would banter back and forth until she was able to complete her task. When she left all would be quiet again.

Often Jack would wait for Ruth in the common room or outside when he knew that she would be mowing the lawn or watering the plants. This proved to be much more fun for her as she had the ultimate weapon, the water hose.

Though Jack loved giving Ruth a hard time, if she ever found herself to be in a tight spot he was always just as quick to give her a helping hand. He had been in the cleaning business for quite a few years and he still knew a few tricks of the trade. He often helped her with vacuum cleaner belts and other such small things that often go awry in that line of work. After we moved away from Winnipeg, I ran into Ruth and she commented that she missed Jack's sense of humor and the way he used to liven the place up.

Jack was a great encourager. After we were married, we continued to live in the same seniors' building in my small suite. We had a tenants' association to help govern the complex. One year I was nominated for president. Jack was really the one most qualified for the job, but I was the one nominated. He had all the books on how to hold a meeting, how to establish a quorum, and all things relevant to conducting business. He had been president of a curling club, of a singles club, and of his own wrestling club. He was the one with experience due to his years with Toastmasters. I knew none of these things. So when I was nominated I was a bit concerned. I was not sure how he would take it.

He, however, did not let it get to him. Instead he dragged out his books and started to educate me on the rules of how to run a meeting and how to do all things presidential. Once the vote was taken and I had won, he got up to announce to everyone that he was the only one privileged enough to sleep with the president. He totally erased any tension that I might have felt. I served as president for three years and he proudly stood behind me all that time. Whenever I would lead a Bible study or later, when I became a deacon in the First Baptist church in Portage, he always affirmed me and proudly told people about the role in which his wife served.

Often Jack would issue me a challenge and then encourage me to continue until I had accomplished it. This was true in just about every area of my life: in art, music, Bible study and church life, our marriage, and in the writing of this book. He taught me to stretch myself outside of my comfort zone and to become something more than what I presently was.

After we were married, my first artistic endeavors were photography and creating my own greeting cards. Frequently, he would sneak out one of my completed projects that he particularly liked and proudly show it around. I found many of these when I was going through his books. I guess he felt that he needed to preserve them for posterity.

Several years after we were married he encouraged me to start painting, and then gave me tips on how to improve. Without this, I never would have started. I had been working on a lighthouse for almost a year and never could get it quite right. One day he came up to me and said it was almost perfect. "Almost" was not what I wanted to hear, and he knew it. The lighthouse was fine, the water was fine, the sky was great, but the rocks on the shoreline were missing something. He looked at it and looked at it and then he suggested that I add a few more rocks up higher on the shore and to darken them and make them very jagged. I accepted his suggestion and it turned out to both of our satisfaction. One of Jack's favorite lines was, "It needs depth." He knew what the picture needed even if he could never have put it there himself. His hands just could not transfer on to paper what his brain imagined.

When I was finished a painting I would snap a picture of it, and then Jack would take it out and show it around. He loved to show off my work. Once when we had gone out to a restaurant in Portage La Prairie, he asked me if he could see some of these snapshots that I usually carried with me. I had no knowledge of his intentions. After we had ordered, he got up and approached the owner with whom he was already acquainted. He asked him if he would consider hanging any of my paintings in his restaurant. The owner came back to the table with Jack and stated, "See that blank wall over there. It is all yours." We hung three paintings on that wall and then Jack told the owner that we had another one that would look great by the washrooms. The owner agreed. It was kind of the understanding at the time that they would hang there on consignment.

Before I moved away, I asked the owner what I should do with the pictures now that Jack had passed away and I was leaving town. He told me that if I would write on each painting, "In memory of Jack Ward" I could leave them there indefinitely. With a silver pen I inscribed in the corner of each painting, "Donated to...in Memory of Jack Ward". The owner was more concerned about honoring the promoter of the artwork than he was in promoting the artist. I was so proud of my husband that day. They all knew who was responsible for those paintings hanging in their restaurant. And I knew who was responsible for helping me to discover my talents and reach my goals.

Jack was also very effective as a promoter. When he got behind something it was usually a success. This was evidenced by his years promoting his own wrestling club, as well as the square dances. This characteristic would follow him into his later years.

For some time, we had been conducting Bible studies and having Christian movies in the common room of the seniors' building where we lived. There was some opposition to this. It seems that the main contention was these events brought in people from outside the building and prevented some of the residents from utilizing the room. The decision to discontinue the Bible studies and movie nights had been all but made when Jack went to work. He went to the building management and reminded them that Friday night bingos brought in a lot of extra people who were not residents. He stated that if a Bible study and movies were not allowed, that he would at once start a petition to have outsiders excluded from bingo nights. But nobody messes with bingo. Nothing was shut down that day.

Whenever we held a fundraiser garage sale, it was Jack who took it upon himself to be the chief advertiser. He would walk all around the neighborhood posting signs and telling everybody he met about the sale. This was his job and he felt comfortable doing it.

There were other duties that he took upon himself. If we had a BBQ for the tenants, it was Jack who usually barbecued the hotdogs and hamburgers. He felt that this job belonged to the husband of the president.

He also felt a bit like a night watchman for our building. We were one of the younger couples in the complex, and so Jack took it upon himself to go around at night and check all the doors. Sometimes he would be missing from our suite for a considerable time and I would go downstairs to find him sitting in the lounge and looking out the window into the dark. He knew if there were drug deals going down at the high school across the street and he saw the comings and goings of big limos that picked up and dropped off kids there at night. All of this activity bothered him, especially because there wasn't really anything that he could do about it. He just hated seeing the kids involved in so much unhealthy activity. Years previous he had initiated a junior wrestling club in order to prevent the youth of his neighborhood from getting involved in such dangerous doings. Now a new generation of kids faced the same kind of dangers and there was nothing that he could do to help any of them.

Jack was a good husband to me. He filled my house with stuff, but even more important, he filled my life with joy. He was my greatest critic and yet my greatest encourager and supporter. Whether in my painting, my music, my work at church, or when I thought my world was falling apart because of yet another cancer diagnosis, he always seemed to know exactly what to say to keep me on track.

I remember when he found an old stringless guitar at a garage sale. He brought it home and stood it behind a chair in our living room. He said that some day he would learn to play it. Once in a while someone would stop in, notice the guitar, and ask who played it. He would reply that he did, but that he could only do so because there were "no strings attached". He could imagine himself playing it and that seemed good enough for him.

As long as Jack owned the guitar no music actually came out of it. But then a young man in our church expressed a desire to learn how to play guitar. Jack gave it to him and never looked back. He was just happy that the young man would soon be playing it in church. What a blessing to be able to give it to him with "no strings attached". That so well defines the way that Jack lived most of his life.

Jack did not possess the ability to put something on paper or canvas, nor could he play any kind of musical instrument. However, he could see or hear when things were not quite right.

Though he could not himself correct these things, he could often point in a direction not previously seen. He always felt that it was better to promote someone else than to stand in their way and hinder them. It is a real gift to sit on the sidelines and cheer somebody else on to success or to stand in the shadows and push someone else into the spotlight. Jack had that gift.

One thing that I did notice about Jack is that he had a very difficult time saying that he was sorry. He could be pressured into saying it, but you really don't like to receive that kind of an apology too often. He was adamant that we don't go to bed angry, so sometimes he would make a blanket unspecific apology just to cover things in general. Again, this is not a highly desirable kind of apology.

In time I came to realize something that did me better service than a grudging apology. If I were to point out a behavior that offended me or if he was proven wrong on some subject, he would graciously give in and change the behavior or correct his erroneous statement. I soon came to appreciate the fact that, though he could not bring himself to say, "I'm sorry", his actions proved that he was. He would not do the same thing over again but actually worked at changing those things that he knew bothered me.

Chapter 14 Flying High

We soon came to realize that if we were to survive as a couple we needed to find another place to live. One of the reasons that Jack sat in the lounge in the evenings was because our apartment was really too small for the both of us. He felt cramped in our small one bedroom apartment. He needed space where he could store all the things he had collected and continued to collect. He needed room where he could spread his arms, write, and "contemplate life". This is what he called those times when he would talk to himself. It was his way of processing life; of thinking things through to the point where they made sense to him. In an effort to accommodate him, we made a request to rent an additional smaller suite. They refused our request.

Another consideration was Jack's voice. He believed in communication and usually did so with great animation and volume. Chemo had nearly silenced him, but now his big voice had returned. People were starting to complain that they could hear him all over the building. And the fact that he talked almost constantly was just too much. I would remind them about the terrible silence he had experienced when he couldn't talk at all, but that did little to resolve the situation. It helped that he was kind and that he was funny, but we definitely needed to find a solution.

Finally we found a 3 bedroom duplex at Southport about 90 kilometers west of Winnipeg.

Southport is a decommissioned Canadian Forces airbase just a few minutes south of Portage la Prairie. Here we would have room to spread out and move around a bit. We moved in April 2007. At last Jack was set free to fly.

Jack had lived in Winnipeg since he was five years old, the only life he remembered. But now he was finally living. He often wrote about how these last years were the best in his life. He loved every day he had there. He thought that life could not get any better than this. This came through so loud in his writings. In several books he wrote about having but one regret. Why did it take him so long to arrive at this place in his life?

Often when I gaze out a window or hear birds singing in the trees I am reminded of how Jack loved the outdoors. He could dig in the dirt, plant things, and make a garden. We grew beautiful tomatoes and luscious raspberries in our little plot. I picked saskatoons and strawberries. This was not for Jack. He didn't have the patience to pick anything. But together we canned, and pickled, and froze fruits and berries and vegetables, plenty for ourselves and enough to give away. In return we would receive more fresh produce which we would can and pickle and freeze. To Jack, this was real living.

In addition to the vegetable garden, Jack created a couple of rock gardens. To this he added driftwood that he had picked up at the Spillway. The Spillway is a part of the Assiniboine River

Floodway, also known as the Portage Diversion, that was built to minimize damage during flood years. It was always a lovely place to visit. It was a beautiful spot for picnics. We often went for walks on trails through the bushes. We even did a bit of rock climbing. There were also wild raspberries and chokecherries to pick. And here Jack got all of the rocks and driftwood for his rock gardens.

On one of our trips to the Spillway, I picked up a piece of driftwood to help me over the rough spots on our walk. It was such a comfortable stick that I decided to take it home. I sanded it down, varnished it, put a rubber tip on the end and wrapped tape on the handle. It became the cane I still use. That planted a seed. I would go back and get more driftwood for walking sticks.

When Jack went to the hospital for the last time, he left the cane I had made for him beside the bathroom door. It stood there until the day I moved. I cried every time I walked past it and saw it standing there, unclaimed. He had placed it there the day that he left our home for the last time. I knew that I needed to move it, but I just couldn't. Then one day it dawned upon me what I should do. I picked it up and walked next door and presented it to our neighbor. Al and Barb Klippenstein had been not just neighbors, but friends. They were godly folks who had always encouraged us along the way. I knew that Al would be the right owner.

The more that there was to do outdoors, the less time was spent collecting varied mementos indoors. Jack lived for those summer days. When I reflected upon how short his life might yet be, I was so glad that we had made the move to Southport. Here it didn't matter if he didn't know which one was his right hand and which one was his left.

Chapter 15 The Return of the Big "C"

In May of 2008, Jack turned seventy. As he came to this milestone, he decided that now was the time he should be baptized. He wanted to have his birthday party and baptism on the same Sunday. We planned to have a huge party at our house after the baptism. We planned it for outdoors, but then it rained all day. We had asked everybody to bring lawn chairs, and now we had to find room for them indoors. Somehow we managed to move things around until we had space to seat forty people all at the same time.

May was also the month that Jack was diagnosed with prostate cancer. I was sure that was to be the end of the road for us. For some reason this cancer depressed me more than any other one before then or since. Jack did not seem to be one bit worried about the news of cancer again. He had developed a deep faith in God and he reminded me more than once that God had brought him through this before and he could do it again. Jack was ever the positive one. He was always able to be a great encouragement to me. They loved him at the cancer support group. He never let an opportunity go by without telling someone of his cancer and how the power of prayer and the grace of God had played a very real part in his healing and his being alive.

It was at this time that we decided to change churches. I had no idea how much Jack would grow spiritually during our time at First Baptist. Jack found this new church to be a place where he was accepted and respected just the way he was. Here Jack could learn at his own pace. And here too, he was welcome to stand up and say what was on his mind when it came time for sharing during praise and worship. Before coming to First Baptist, Jack always kind of felt like all the work of the Lord had either already been done or was being done by people who knew more about it than he did. Now he realized that each person is just as important as the next, and that we all have a job no matter how small.

This was a revelation to Jack. It caused him to step out and take a leadership role in areas that he believed suited him. When I started a women's group, Jack thought that if it was good for the ladies, it would be good for the men also. So he started a men's group. From what I could gather, they really had a lot of fun. After they had a devotional, there were many stories told. From day one, Jack's best friend was Henry Carlson. These two were definitely a bit "off the wall". When they got together they really did act crazy. Often they would go to a restaurant and cut up so bad, joking around and giving the waitress such a bad time that she would bring the wrong orders to the wrong people. We made such wonderful friends at this church.

While being loved on by these people, Jack truly bloomed. Here he felt appreciated for who he was and what he brought to the church. It was after we joined a couple's Bible study that I heard Jack pray out loud for the first time. I nearly fell out of my chair. Later, at a Christmas dinner, my kids nearly fell out of theirs when they first heard him pray. This was certainly a different Jack than the one they had known all their lives.

From time to time Jack would remind me of the question that he asked after his first cancer had gone into remission. Since God had saved him from both physical and spiritual death, what did God want of him? He was slowly coming to understand that God had spared him to fill a place, but even more, he was discovering that what God really wanted from him was his love and devotion. This he was prepared to do. At every opportunity he would give God all the praise and glory for his still being here on planet Earth. He never acted as though he was threatened by whatever anybody else did. He just felt secure in the knowledge that God loved him.

Another big event that took place in 2008 was Jack's decision to get a dog. He said that he wanted a dog that really needed a home. That is why we decided to adopt a dog from a shelter rather than acquire a new puppy. Jack seemed to have a soft spot for things abandoned, maybe because of his own life experiences. And so "Baby" entered our lives, a lap dog for me and a loyal little companion for Jack. They played together and every afternoon they napped together. She gave him one more reason to keep going when the road took another bad turn.

Jack continued to have his health concerns, but soon it was to be my turn again. In 1998 I had had a cancerous kidney removed. In 2007, the year we moved to Southport, I was found to have a genetic condition called a "pancreatic divisum". By the time this was diagnosed it had developed into fatty liver disease. Though this required some adjustment in life style, it was not until 2011 that things took a near deadly turn. I had become so tired and weak that I could barely function. After much testing I was found to have thyroid cancer. Subsequently, I was found to also have a parathyroid tumor. While being treating for these I was given a medication that caused kidney failure in my one remaining kidney. For a time things looked pretty bleak.

This series of events did quite a number on Jack. I was hospitalized two separate times that summer for a week each time. It was then that I appreciated the fact that we had that little dog. He proved to be a real blessing. Jack was very concerned about me, but he also had Baby to take care of. That necessity helped to keep Jack's feet grounded and his mind on something other than my health.

Chapter 16 If I Had Only Known

In April 2012, after a CT scan, the doctor informed us that Jack needed surgery for a large lymph node in his groin area. He looked at us very somberly and I finally perceived that he was expecting some kind of reaction from us. I asked him if that was what he was waiting for. "Well", he replied, "I am kind of waiting for this to register on you." I informed him that we had already experienced all the reactions to cancer that we could muster and that we had no more left. I told him that we had decided to live life one day at a time and so far, by God's grace, we had always come through.

Then Jack asked the unthinkable. The promoters of the Terry Fox Run in Portage La Prairie had asked us, as cancer survivors, if we would do the honor of being the starters for the 2012 run. That meant that Jack would get a chance to speak into a microphone and that he would announce the start. No one could move until he said, "Let the race begin." This intrigued Jack. And besides this, he wanted to give something back.

The surgery was supposed to be performed immediately. What Jack was proposing was that they delay the surgery for a week until after the run. For some reason, they actually went for it.

Jack was elated. In his speech at the starting line he talked more about God and the power of prayer than he did about his past cancers. The local newspaper printed a layout of pictures and included

Jack's address word-for-word.

As we registered for the race, Jack and I presented over $800 that we had raised for cancer research. The promoters said that never in the history of the race in Portage la Prairie had the starters brought in so much money. Being a starter for the Run was considered to be a prestige position and they were not expected to raise that kind of funds. I hope we started a trend.

A week later Jack had surgery. They opened him and closed him right back up again. It seems they had misread the CT scan. The doctors had perceived cancer, but in reality the lump was the netting and scar tissue from a previous hernia operation. He went home the same day.

During an appointment six weeks later the doctor told us that if the lump had been cancer they would not have been able to save him, partially due to the longer wait for surgery. I was so glad that we did not know this before the run. We undoubtedly would have made a different choice and Jack would have missed out on the fun and satisfaction he experienced in the walk. He had actually walked the course around Island Park three times and made a new friend along the way.

There are so many ups and downs in living life with cancer. On the day that we were informed that the decision to delay the surgery could have been a fatal one, we were driving home from Winnipeg when we saw a tree that had been uprooted during a storm. For us it seemed that a storm always preceded the calm; that when life was raging around us, God would always step in and bring peace. As we reflected upon this I began to compose a poem in my mind. When we arrived home I wrote it out.

The Storm Before the Calm

Winds are rushing,
Trees are swaying,
Cattle are lowing,
Dogs are barking,
It feels like a storm.

The winds are roaring,
Trees are thrashing,
Cattle are bawling,
Dogs are howling,
There is a storm.

Lightning flashes
Thunder crashes,
Cattle chased to the stable,
Dogs are under the table,
Hiding from the storm.

The winds are silent,
trees are uprooted,
Livestock is shaken,
Dogs tails are wagging,
The storm has passed,

The meadow is quiet,
There's a rainbow above,
Once again God has shown,
His mighty power,
And then His great Love.

Besides the other cancers, Jack had several different types of skin cancer. None of these were life threatening, but they were a nuisance. It became extremely trying as each one was either surgically removed or burned off with nitro gas or a variety of creams. At one time it seemed that the creams had burned off the outer layer of skin from his entire face. For months at a time he would not go anywhere except to the doctors. He bravely endured all of this without complaining or asking why this was happening to him.

Late 2012 he started to lose blood and had to be taken off his blood thinners. This proved tricky due to his history of strokes. Some miscalculations were made and he developed a major arterial blood clot. Then, when the clot broke loose part of it lodged in his right hand. We went from one hospital to another, back home, and then to another hospital in an effort to resolve this. For a while we thought he would lose the use of his hand. It was always so cold and blue. And the pain was awful. It took three months to finally get this cleared up.

The blood clot was dissolved, but his loss of blood was still not solved. A colonoscopy was scheduled. It came back clear. A CT scan was ordered. It came back clear. A set of x-rays were taken. They all came back clear.

In June of 2013 Jack insisted on having a tenth anniversary party at our church to renew our vows. I hesitated because of all the work, but he really wanted this. Now I am so glad we made the effort. His reasoning was that we might not have another chance to celebrate an anniversary together. Even though nothing conclusive was happening, he was still losing weight. He was actually feeling better than he did on our wedding day as the sore on his bum had been...well, a pain in the rear. But somehow Jack sensed that this anniversary needed to be celebrated.

Ten years. This was a milestone. Jack's first marriage had lasted five years. This was a victory day for him, a day of accomplishment. And he loved every minute of it. When we got married in 2003 we were told that it might be only for a year or two. We could not believe that it had been ten years. As Jack jokingly repeated throughout the day, "If I had known it was going to last this long, I would have taken my vows more seriously."

One thing was certain. We were both fully aware that if God had not been there for both of us through our various cancers and other illnesses, neither one of us would be here to celebrate this event. Not only did we want to celebrate our ten years together, but we also wanted to commemorate the goodness of God and to thank Him for our years together. It had been a miracle from the beginning.

Chapter 17 The End and the Beginning

In September 2013 Jack started to bleed from the rectum. This was a huge warning sign. It had been less than two months since he had had his last colonoscopy. He was sent back to the same surgeon who could not believe what he saw. The tumors could be evidenced from the outside. One more colonoscopy and a biopsy revealed a very aggressive form of rectal cancer. The original rectal cancer that was treated as a bed sore for years had come back to haunt us.

During the biopsy, a muscle was severed which caused Jack to permanently lose bowel control. He was scheduled to get a colostomy bag. Until then he was to wear pull-up underwear pads. We would often joke about the TV commercial for toddler pull-ups, saying of Jack, "He's a big kid now."

On the evening of November 9, while we were waiting for a PET scan and surgery, Jack became disoriented. When we got to the hospital the doctor diagnosed him with a "brain bleed". Apparently with all of his weight loss, his blood thinners were making his blood too thin. The next morning I went in to see him and he did not know who I was or even that he had a wife.

Five days later he got up at night to go to the bathroom by himself. He fell asleep while on the toilet and slid off breaking his hip. This was just so hard to take because it shouldn't have happened.

The railing on his bed had inadvertently been left down and he had gotten up on his own. He had been instructed to call for help when he felt the need to get up, but he decided he could manage on his own. To make matters worse, he was simply put back to bed. I was not called, nor did they send him to X-ray. For the next 13 ½ hours he tried to change positions in bed, to move himself from bed to wheelchair to bathroom, and to accomplish all of the other functions of the morning, all without additional pain medication.

When I arrived in the afternoon I was less than happy. I finally got them to wheel him to X-ray in his wheelchair. Minutes later they came running back for his bed. My worst fears were confirmed. His hip was fractured.

The day of his PET scan appointment arrived and he was sent to Winnipeg by ambulance. The doctor called me with the results. Some of his skin cancers were back, but worse yet, he had thyroid cancer and his prostate and rectal cancer were so intertwined that the machine could no longer differentiate between them. He had reached an inoperable stage and the only thing that they could do for him was to possibly give him a colostomy bag. However, with or without the colostomy, he was headed for palliative care. He also needed to be on stronger doses of pain medications that needed to be monitored closely.

We had planned to do his palliative care at home. But with his broken hip, which they decided not to operate on, this was no longer an option. I requested a private room for him so that he could rest more comfortably and so that I could come and go as I pleased. I also insisted on a comfortable recliner chair to sleep in anytime I decided to stay overnight. The hospital staff informed me that there were no private rooms available. The doctor on staff advised me to transfer him to Winnipeg where there was plenty of palliative space. I much preferred that we stay in Portage where we would be close to home. After much consultation, the hospital finally agreed to give us a private room.

From this point on Jack was confined to bed. He seemed to take this all in stride. This was truly a gift from God. It was not in his nature to sit or lie still for any length of time. He had Attention Deficit and he had always had to move, move, move. Now he had to lie quietly in one place. A nurse suggested an air mattress for which we were deeply thankful. This provided a good deal of comfort. Jack had the most amazing attitude about palliative care. In life he never did anything halfway. He always did everything to the best of his ability. Now, in dying, he felt he needed to finish life as he had lived, with determination and dignity. He did not complain or pity himself. It was important to him that his family and friends see him nobly fight for life and then gracefully yield with honor.

It was during this time that Rev. James Davey, the acting pastor of our church, and his wife Marilyn paid Jack a visit. Jack was having a particularly bad day. He had been in a deep sleep for several hours and could not be roused. The nursing staff was gravely concerned calling it "the death sleep". I needed to go home for a short time to attend to our little dog and take care of some business, so I had asked the Daveys if they could come spend some time with Jack. While sitting by Jack's bedside, Rev. Davey began reading Scripture out loud trusting that Jack would still be able to hear. Suddenly, Jack opened his eyes and started talking a mile a minute, just as if he had not been in a coma-like sleep. Having finished my business and returned to the hospital, I heard him talking as I walked down the hallway towards his room. Much the same thing happened sometime later when Jack was in a similar state and Rev. Davey visited and sang "He the Pearly Gates Will Open".

These were bittersweet days and nights for us. We spent many hours talking about what had been and the many things that we had enjoyed doing together. Jack told me that he had only one real regret. He had already mentioned this several times in his writings, but now he was saying it aloud to me. He wished that we had married sooner and therefore had been able to spend more time together. He felt like he had wasted half his life grieving over the loss of a woman that had been a terrible mistake from the beginning. One day he asked me, "If heaven is so much better, why do I want to stay here?" I asked him what made him feel that way. He responded, "I just hate to leave something so good behind. Before I married you I didn't know that life could be so good." He also didn't want to say good-by to his new enlarged family.

Another thing that bothered him was the fact that I had gone through all of this before with my first husband John. He felt bad that I once again had to sit and watch another husband die. I asked him if he would rather that I went first. To this he gave an adamant "No!" He stated that he would not want to keep living without his wife. I continued by telling him that God in his goodness was sparing him from a life of loneliness, something that he had experienced for far too long before we were married.

Then too he wished that he had started his Christian life sooner. It grieved him that he had had such a short time to witness what God was able to accomplish in a yielded life. He was just beginning to understand what it all meant and now it would soon be over. Twelve years previous he had been given two months to live, but it was then that he found life. He had promised God that if he survived that death sentence he would live for Him the rest of his days. Jack had kept his promise. One day Jack had heard the word "backsliding". He asked me what people meant by that word. I told him it referred to Christians who went back to their old life after having found God. He responded, "Now that's dumb! Why would anyone want to go back to that stuff after they had found something real good?"

For Jack it was always forward, never backward.

We did talk funeral plans and worked out some of the details he would like to have happen. He had certain songs he wanted us to sing, "Count Your Blessings" and "I Come to the Garden Alone". He wanted Len Hart, my brother-in-law to do the service. Len had participated in our wedding over 10 years previous and had officiated at the renewal of our vows just months before. He wanted Dean Lutz to do the eulogy and Cecil Brown to read the obituary. He also requested that Rev. James Davey sing a solo, "He the Pearly Gates Will Open".

Soon it would be Christmas. Jack was resolute that he would not die before Christmas. At first I thought this was because he loved the season so much. But then he said it was because he did not want me to have to remember his death in all my Christmases to come. He knew what a lonely time Christmas could be and did not want the memory of his passing to be added to my loneliness each year.

Jack never quit writing, even in the hospital when his strength was waning, until the day before he passed away. In his last little notebook are written these thoughts, most of them written while he was in the hospital. Again I will use his spelling and large capital letters:

"NEVER DRIVE FASTER THAN YOUR GUARDIAN ANGEL CAN FLY". (I wish he had that one before he towed me down the highway at 100 km/h.) And yes, this time he spelt it all correctly.

*DON'T TAKE LIFE TO CERIOUSLY, NO ONE GETS OUT
ALIVE.
TREAT YOU WIFE LIKE A "THOROUGHBRED" AND SHE
WON'T TURN INTO AN "OLD NAG".
WHAT WAS YOUR BEST DAY (GOD)SAVING MY LIFE AND
LETTING ME TAKE A WIFE.
TIME IS RUNNING OUT. ENJOY EACH OTHER , EACH
ONE DAY AT A TIME. AND ENJOY ALL THE GOOD
THINGS IN LIF (LIKE) SUNSHINE, FAMILY, FRIENDS.
QUESTION, HOW ARE YOU TODAY? BETTER THAN I
BEEN FOR EACH DAY IN MY LIFE IS AN IMPROVEMENT.
TODAY I HAVE BEEN BLESSED BY GOD, (HYMN) OH HOW
I LOVE JESUS.
I AM THANKFUL FOR ALL THINGS, FOR IN
EVERYTHING I GIVE THANKS, 1 THESALONIANS 5:8.
LIFE; BETTER UNDERSTANDING OF WHO GOD IS, AND
HOW HE RELATES TO THE PEOPLE HE CREATED.*

This last line he wrote in the morning after a
night that I spent at home. He was lonely and a bit
worried that he would pass away when I was not
there. In this frame of mind he asked God to show
him peace and beauty. He was granted his request
in the form of a vision where an angel took him all
around the world and showed him what peace and
beauty and love looked like. He was given a tour of
the outside of heaven and when he inquired if he
could see inside he was told it wasn't time yet. He
was very impressed with the overwhelming sense of
peace. He said that he was even shown his old
wrestling club, but there was no fighting there, only
peace. In the morning he asked me where God had
gotten so much glass. Personally, I think he saw the
purest of gold, but I told him that if God created

glass he could use as much of it as He wanted to.

The nights that I did not stay at the hospital Jack would always call me early in the morning to say "Good Morning". He would usually begin by saying something flowery and then tell me how thankful he was that God had allowed us to have another day to spend together. One morning he dialed the wrong number by mistake. A strange lady answered and wanted to know who he was saying that stuff to her in the morning. Jack said, "Oops! I'm sorry. Wrong number." Then he hung up. I don't even want to guess what that lady was thinking.

My daughters spent as much time as they could at the hospital with us. If I called them and told them that Jack was not having a good day, they would come as soon as their husbands could work themselves free. Sometime they would come the same day. At other times it would be the next day. Wanda stayed over with us on many nights. Twyla came bearing Christmas goodies and decorations. She knew how much Jack loved Christmas. And since he once played Santa Claus for her, it was only fitting that she now played Santa Claus for him. She also knew that I would not be decorating our home for Christmas, so this would most likely be the only Christmas that I had as well.

Before Christmas, our grandchildren all came out to see Jack. Twyla and John brought their three, Arron, Whitney, and Jennifer, and Wanda and Tim brought their two, David and Carrie. Since

Jack had no family, it was good for my girls to step in and make him feel family closeness. They phoned him, hugged him when they entered the room, and from time to time the whole gang would gather around the bed and take family pictures.

Our "adopted" kids from church, Dale and Janet, also came frequently. Once, Janet sat with Jack while Dale took me out for coffee as a respite. Another time Sheila, a lady from our church, lined up some palliative care people to come and spend time with Jack so that I could get away for awhile. This worked well for me as there were times I needed to tend to everyday business. Often I would just run home, take care of our little dog, shower and change, and then run right back. As soon as I left, I could hardly wait to get back. These times did not work out quite so well for Jack. He often gave these people a bit of a hard time because he wanted me to be with him. When he came to realize that he had been out of sorts he would always apologize.

The winter of 2012-2013 was desperately cold in Manitoba and yet my van always started. It would sit in the open parking lot at the hospital for long hours without being plugged in, often overnight, and yet I would go out, turn the key, and it would run like a charm. One day Sheila said that my van was anointed by the Lord because it always started without hesitation. This was just one of the many things with which God blessed me during this time.

People came and went. Some brought

goodies, some brought music, and some just dropped in to say a quick hello. My cousin Lillian came very often and frequently stayed for hours. Once we sat and watched a whole comedy show together. Lillian had never seen Victor Borge before. He is a piano virtuoso who is known for his comedic routines. We laughed so hard that the nurses looked in to see how so much fun could be had in a palliative care room.

Jack's room did not have the atmosphere of someone who was dying. Often people would come in somberly, wondering how they could encourage Jack and they would leave having been encouraged themselves. Jack kept on telling his stories, trying to bless people by cheering them up. He still wanted to hear people laugh around him. When his friend Maurice came in, he would throw his arms in the air and literally welcome Maurice with open arms. Then they would proceed to throw funny stories and jokes around. Maurice could not figure out how a man who knew he was dying could be so happy. This comment came from many people. Jack continued to tell stories until the day before he passed away. Sometimes the details of the story were all messed up and sometimes he fell asleep while telling it, but his spirits were almost always high. When he did have a bad day, he would generally sleep through it. This was likely due to the pain control medication that he was being given.

A few days before Christmas the doctor told us that Jack would probably only make it a few more days. When he came back after Christmas he could not believe that Jack was still hanging on and still talking and joking. The scene repeated itself after the new year.

On Christmas Eve day Jack wanted me to go and play Christmas music on the other wards in the hospital. When we were cleaning out my father's apartment at his death in 2008, I had laid claim to his harmonicas. Since then I had been teaching myself to play. Respecting Jack's request, I decided that the dialysis unit would be a good place to start. From there I moved to the Extended Care Unit. Even now, he wanted to spread Christmas cheer to all those within his circle. He said that even though things looked grim and we seemed to have little to celebrate, we still had the birth of Jesus to rejoice in and that was enough.

That evening, our girls and their families got together to have their Christmas meal. Afterwards they put together a full dinner and brought it to the hospital for us the next day. They brought so much that, along with the goodies our friends were bringing us, we had far more than enough for ourselves. We decided to do up trays of dainties to share with the nursing staff who were working so hard over the holidays. We did the same on New Year's Day.

After we welcomed in the New Year, Jack found a new goal to hang on to. My youngest sister Shirley and her husband Dan were coming from British Columbia to attend a family gathering. They were scheduled to arrive on the 9th. I didn't believe that he would make it until then. But he was determined, and not only did he get to see them, but he hung on well beyond their return home.

It was during these last days that my sister Mary-Anne phoned and told me that she had had a vision of Jack doing a beautiful Davidic dance in heaven. She wanted to perform this at Jack's funeral, but it didn't work out. She performed it later for me, and I wish that there was some way that I could show on these pages how it looked. Jack loved to dance, and we knew that one day very soon he would be dancing again. This time, however, he would be dancing before the Lord in complete health.

When I agreed to marry Jack I had determined in my heart to honor him. He had gone into a physical and financial tailspin when he first became sick. Now I wanted to treat him in such a way that the dignity that he had had when he promoted wrestling, called square dances, and ran the night shift at the bank would be restored. More than that, I wanted to add a new dimension to his life. I wanted to fill his life with love. I wanted him to mature in his spiritual walk. And I wanted to do all that I could to keep him as healthy as possible. That was my goal. Now I could see that this had been accomplished, but that instead of me doing it all, we had done it together. Jack had worked hard on his own to find that which he had lost and in the process he had filled my heart, life, and home with joy and love.

I had never told Jack about my goal. But his determination to fulfill the promises he had made to God, to marry me and provide a good life for us and to get to know God better, also worked to win his self-respect back. He never looked back at his old life. He was always faithful to God and to me and thankful to God for all his blessings. It was evident that we had worked together to reestablish his dignity and to command a new respect.

Jack said that he was hanging on for me, but really it was because he had fallen in love with his life. He said that the last 10½ years had been the best years of his life, and he felt that they had been far too short.

As the end neared, Jack inquired of the nurse if I could play my harmonica through the night. He said that the last thing that he wanted to hear was me playing gospel songs. The nurse responded by saying that I could play until 11:30 pm.

Sunday, January 19, 2014, the night before he passed, I noticed that both of his cheek bones were cold. Something in me told me that he would not awaken with us the next morning. Wanda had decided to stay through the night with us. Towards the middle of the night she awoke to his cry of pain and to his thrashing around in the bed. I was so sound asleep that she had to come close and yell in my ear to wake me. Then she called the nurse who came running with a needle of pain medication. I told her that he had said that he wanted to leave this world with the sounds of my harmonica in his ears. Though it was 2:30 am, she stated, "Then play now!" As I played his two favorite hymns, "He Touched Me" and "Count Your Blessings", he slipped silently into the presence of his Savior in his eternal home.

Then something miraculous occurred. When my cousin Lillian had said goodnight to him the previous evening, she too felt that he would not make it through the night. She had said, "Jack, I will see you in the morning, one way or another." After she had gone to bed, she was awakened at 2:30 with an urge to go to the washroom. As she walked down the hallway she saw Jack floating out of her apartment in a white robe. He had come to say goodbye to her. I was impressed with the fact that God had already supplied him with a white robe of righteousness. He had left his own clothes and his body behind and had gone home in a garment that the Bible says all believers will wear in heaven (Rev 7:9; Isa 61:10; Zec 3:4).

Jack had twelve years to prepare for this moment. He was faithful in his preparation and God proved Himself faithful to Jack. I know beyond a shadow of a doubt that I will see Jack again when it comes my turn to cross over beyond what we call death. All the pain that he endured and that we experienced together will be worth it. My beloved Jack has gone home to Jesus where there will be no more tears or pain or suffering. He fought a good fight and he finished his course. He was willing to learn from those who were willing to teach him. The skills that he had developed to overcome his learning disabilities sometimes dictated that he had to learn things on his own. I often did not know how to teach him various Christian concepts, so it had to be just him and God. He accepted the challenge and now he is home with the One he loves and with the One who loved him.

I would like to include Jack's prayer from his 23rd consecutive Christmas letter:

Jack's Prayer

Lord I am praying to you today.
I am not asking You for anything.
I have my wife, my family, my friends, my church, and my good neighbors.
This is as good as it gets.
It doesn't get any better than this.
It's my favorite time of day,
when I can come aside to talk to You.
I want to thank You for being there for me all through my cancer years and for all the blessings You have granted me.
I have trusted you to be my Lord and Savior, and have accepted the challenge of living for you for the rest of my life.
You have become my Heavenly Father and you will walk with me through all the rest of my life to follow.
Thank You for the freedom from the power of

sin, and the promise of eternal life.   Jack

Several times I have made reference to First Corinthians 13 and to FAITH, HOPE, and LOVE. These were important concepts to Jack and he cited this passage many times in his notebooks. He even wrote it out in its entirety. He always collected things that he thought would be of benefit to him and to others. Since he took the time to write it out in full, I believe that he meant for others to read it. I would also like to write it out for you, especially for those who may not have read it in its original context.

1 Corinthians 13 (NIV)

12 31bAnd yet I will show you the most excellent way. 13 1If I speak in the tongues of men or of angels, but do not have love, I am only a resounding gong or a clanging cymbal. 2If I have the gift of prophecy and can fathom all mysteries and all knowledge, and if I have a faith that can move mountains, but do not have love, I am nothing. 3If I give all I possess to the poor and give over my body to hardship, but do not have love, I gain nothing.
4Love is patient, love is kind. It does not envy, it does not boast, it is not proud. 5It is not rude, it is not self-seeking, it is not easily angered, it keeps no record of wrongs. 6Love does not delight in evil but

rejoices with the truth. ⁷It always protects, always trusts, always hopes, always perseveres.

⁸Love never fails. But where there are prophecies, they will cease; where there are tongues, they will be stilled; where there is knowledge, it will pass away. ⁹For we know in part and we prophesy in part, ¹⁰but when perfection comes, the imperfect disappears. ¹¹When I was a child, I talked like a child, I thought like a child, I reasoned like a child. When I became a man, I put the ways of childhood behind me. ¹²For now we see only a poor reflection as in a mirror; then we shall see face to face. Now I know in part; then I shall know fully, even as I am fully known.

¹³And now these three remain: faith, hope and love. But the greatest of these is love.

As I come to the end of the story, I am made very much aware that this could not have happened without Jack. First of all, it is his story. I only play a role in it. Secondly, it was Jack that gave me the courage to start what has turned out to be a rather large project. He was my inspiration to tackle that which I considered too big for me to do. He endorsed it and he promoted it, much like he did many other things throughout his life. It was Jack who gathered and collected materials for this project and then for years talked it into being.

This is something that I feel that Jack and I accomplished together. Again, it is his story. I simply organized it and put into writing those things he wanted to say but was unable.

Thank you, Jack. I will love you forever for the encouragement you were to me, not only in completing your story, but in facing the many pitfalls in life that we endured together. I will always love you for all the things you meant to me. Thank you for all the stories, the write-ups, and the almost constant chatter. Mostly, thank you for your love and the many tributes you wrote to me.

I will see you again, my dear husband, and I know you will be waiting there for me "just inside the Eastern Gate". I know you are up there dancing, and that someday we will be up there dancing together. I know that you can now see Jesus in person, and have no more need for windows or pencil sharpeners to help you learn. You are experiencing God's grace, face to face. What a glorious day that will be when together Jesus we will see!

I don't know where this will go from here. I have done my part. My prayer is that everyone who reads this book will be encouraged to fight through any disabilities that they may have and all of the illnesses or diseases that they may encounter, and that in the end they, like Jack, will be drawn closer into a life with God.

Acknowledgements

There are so many people I need to thank. There were so many people that attended to us in so many ways. First and foremost I would like to thank my two daughters and their husbands, Wanda and Tim Hovey and Twyla and John Budz. Wanda, thank you for staying up with me during so many nights in those final days; and Twyla, thanks so much for the frequent phone calls, the meals out, and for bringing Christmas with all its decorations and goodies to the palliative care unit. You all made life so much easier.

And to my grandchildren David, Carrie, Arron, Whitney and Jennifer who came to visit Grandpa Jack and by doing so made each day a day to be remembered. Thank you David and Carrie for helping me move when that time came, and Carrie for watching our little dog when we couldn't.

To my siblings and their spouses: Wilbert & Della Unger, Cliff & Linda Unger, Eva & Herman Penner, Earl & Mary Unger, Mary-Anne & Len Hart, and Shirley & Dan Wiebe. Thank you for your great support and the ways you respected Jack during his dying days. He was very fond of each of you and did not want to leave us to grieve his passing at Christmas time, so he waited and waited until into January. And to my cousin Lillian Unger, you are like a sister to me.

To our church family at First Baptist Church - Portage la Prairie who did more for us than I can possibly mention, for rides and meals and visits and prayer and supports of all kinds -- Dale & Janet Lenton, our "adopted" kids, Rev. James & Marilyn Davey, John & Audrey Bender, Cecil Brown, Henry & Doedy Carlson, Dean & Margaret Lutz, Blaine & Diane MacFarlane, Margaret Schnurr, Melba Morrey, Maurice Mould, Gerald & Joyce Verhoeve, Jim & Sheila Knox & their two children.

To those who brought music -- Ruth & Andre Seguin and my cousin and his wife, Jeff & Barbara Guenther.

To our good friends and neighbours in Portage la Prairie and South Port -- our friends of so many years, Ed and Carole Plachner and their daughter and grandchildren, Peter & Sharla and Derrick & Ashley Martindale. Thanks for all the Tim Horton's runs. To Raymond and Carlene Walmsley, and our neighbours Ivan & Barb Foster who saw to it that our lawn was mown and garden tilled in the summer and our driveway cleared in the winter, and Al & Barb Klippenstein who were great encouragers.

A special thank you to all of Jack's friends who were attentive to Jack to the very end, who shared some of their memories of Jack and who allowed their names to be printed in this book -- from his school days: Nora Steward, Debra Grey (Hummel), Bob Neufield, and his oldest school buddy Art Cheadle;   from his wrestling days: John and Barry Searcy, Claire Morden and his wife Jane, Wayne Matthews, and Tom Emms; from his dancing days: Alva & June Cowan, Al Hammerton and his wife Evelyn who taught Jack how to polka, and Cheryl Jensen.

I would again like to thank my brother-in-law Len Hart, his wife Mary-Anne, my sister, and their daughter Cara, who all helped to edit and re-edit and rewrite and proof and re-proof this text. I know that this was more of a daunting task than you had anticipated.

Last, but definitely not least, a huge thank you to the staff in the palliative care unit at Portage District General Hospital. All of you, the medical, housekeeping, and dietary staff were all wonderful. One person that I cannot fail to mention is Gayle from housekeeping. She was always there, cheering us up, laughing with us, and crying with us. She even came to my house once after Jack had passed away. Never under estimate the importance of the support staff in the hospital. They often go above and beyond the fulfillment of their duties to give the personal touch. Thank you to all the Gayles for performing what is so often a thankless job.

Please forgive me if I left anyone out. It sure was not my intention. But it happens to us, especially when there are so many that enter your life on a day-to-day basis and make a deposit of joy in your life. Each one of you was so important to Jack and myself. My prayer is that that this book can be seen as evidence of our gratitude.

To God be the glory! Amen.

Printed in the United States
By Bookmasters